Copyright © 2020 by Clifford Publishing, UK

All rights reserved. No part of this book may be reprinted or reproduced or utilised in any form or by any electronic, mechanical, or other means, now known or hereafter invented, including photocopying and recording, or in any information storage or retrieval system, without permission in writing from the publishers.

First Printing, 2020

British Library Cataloguing-in-Publication Data

A catalogue record for this book is available from the British Library

ISBN 978-1-913558-01-7

Clifford Publishing

1 Dock Road, London

United Kingdom, E16 1AH

www.cliffordpub.com

DATA TRANSLATION

Jie Fang
Jing Li

2020

Preface

Modern software always has a multiple-level hierarchical architecture and complex structure, and it also involves a variety of third-party modules and tools. Data translating and interfacing therefore play an import role among different modules and tools. A model base data translation is described in the book for the purpose of correctness, complete and consistency on both syntax and semantic levels.

An information model is conventionally built in order to capture the requirements and structure of information at a conceptual level. This book explores ways of exploiting information models. In this particular case, the intent is to investigate how information models may be mapped in order to automate the process of generating data translators.

The work focuses on an examination of issues relating to the development of data translators, which generate output in the 2D graphical domain. The book describes the development of two data translators, which provide appropriate case studies. An information model describing the target of the translation was created and formal mappings were developed between two other information models and the target model. The mappings were then evaluated through the manual development of two translators to implement the mappings.

The initial research into model based data translation was based on a concrete case: Translation and representation of 2D graphical data. Two translators, a Gerber-To-SVG translator and an AGS-To-SVG translator, were created. They are two different classes of translators. Though they are not the only types of translator that people want to produce, they are representative and the solutions drawn from them may be useful in the development of other types of translator.

The Gerber-To-SVG translator and the AGS-To-SVG translator were experiments for testing and evaluating the model based approach. The issues that emerged during the development of these two translators have not been fully addressed, but they provide some clues to future research work.

An assessment of some of the issues that must be considered when mappings are to be used in order to automate the data translation process was then carried out and is reported in the book.

This book was composed by Dr. Jie FANG and Ms. Jing LI. Dr. Jie FANG have been architect in multiple domains, such as Banking and Insurance for twenty years and his research interests includes AI, Information Modelling, Natural Language Processing and Knowledge Graph. He was awarded Doctoral Degree from University of Manchester in 2005. Ms. Jing LI had been teaching English in Shanghai High School for twelve years, and also edited the English text book for Chinese Secondary school in Oxford Publishing House. She is a linguistic, focusing on Corpus, English learning. Ms. Jing LI was awarded Master degree from Shanghai Jiaotong University in 2005.

Table of Contents

CHAPTER 1 INTRODUCTION 1

    1.1 INTRODUCTION TO DATA TRANSLATION 1

    1.2 MODEL BASED DATA TRANSLATION 1

    1.3 MODEL MAPPING 2

    1.4 CONTENTS OF THE BOOK 4

CHAPTER 2 INFORMATION MODELLING AND THE USE OF EXPRESS 5

    2.1 INFORMATION MODELS 5

    2.2 THE FEATURES OF AN INFORMATION MODEL 5

        2.2.1 Objects 5

        2.2.2 Attributes 6

        2.2.3 Relationships between objects 6

        2.2.4 Constraints on objects and their relationships 7

    2.3 WHAT AN INFORMATION MODEL IS NOT 7

    2.4 WAYS OF DESCRIBING AN INFORMATION MODEL 7

        2.4.1 UML 8

        2.4.2 IDEF1X 9

    2.5 THE EXPRESS LANGUAGE AND ITS EXPRESS-G GRAPHICAL REPRESENTATION 10

        2.5.1 SCHEMA 12

        2.5.2 Data types 13

        2.5.3 ENTITY 16

        2.5.4 Attributes 16

        2.5.5 Generalization/specialization 16

    2.6 CONCLUSIONS 17

CHAPTER 3 INFORMATION MODEL MAPPING 18

    3.1 INFORMATION MODEL MAPPING 18

    3.2 REQUIREMENTS ON MODEL MAPPINGS 19

    3.3 INFORMATION MODEL MAPPING LANGUAGES 20

        3.3.1 The EXPRESS-X language 21

3.4 EMM MODEL MAPPING REPRESENTATION 23
    3.4.1 Viewing the mapping from two levels 23
    3.4.2 The structure of EMM 24
    3.4.3 Mapping Unit 26
    3.4.4 Relationship between mapping units 27
    3.4.5 Comparison between the EMM and EXPRESS-X 27
3.5 THE MODEL MAPPING METHODS IN THE UML FAMILY AND THE XML FAMILY. 27
3.6 CONCLUSIONS 27

CHAPTER 4 SVG AND ITS INFORMATION MODEL 29

4.1 INTRODUCTION TO SVG 29
4.2 THE STRUCTURE OF AN SVG MODEL 29
4.3 SOME OTHER MODELLING ISSUES 31
    4.3.1 ABSTRACT SUPERTYPES 31
    4.3.2 INVERSE attributes and existence dependencies 31
4.4 SVG_GEOMETRY_MODEL 31
    4.4.1 Basic geometry data types 31
    4.4.2 Basic Shape 34
    4.4.3 Path 35
    4.4.4 Text 36
    4.4.5 Transformation of graphic elements 37
4.5 SVG_STRUCTURE_MODEL 37
    4.5.1 Structure of SVG document fragments 37
    4.5.2 Reuse mechanism of SVG 39
4.6 SVG_PRESENTATION_MODEL 39
    4.6.1 Container attributes 39
    4.6.2 Paint attributes 40
    4.6.3 Graphic attributes 40
    4.6.4 Marker attributes 40
    4.6.5 Font selection attributes 41
    4.6.6 Text content attributes 42

- 4.6.7 Text attributes 43
- 4.7 SVG_INTERACTIVITY_MODEL 43
  - 4.7.1 Script 43
  - 4.7.2 Graphic Element Events 44
  - 4.7.3 Document Events 44
  - 4.7.4 Animation Events 45
- 4.8 SVG_ANIMATION_MODEL 45
- 4.9 SVG_EXTERNAL_SOURCE_MODEL 45
  - 4.9.1 The terminal user's information 46
  - 4.9.2 Other referenced information 46

CHAPTER 5 WORKED EXAMPLE 1: GERBER-TO-SVG TRANSLATOR 47

- 5.1 INTRODUCTION TO THE GERBER FORMAT 47
  - 5.1.1 The structure of the Gerber format 47
  - 5.1.2 Two coding formats for the Gerber data 48
- 5.2 INTRODUCTION TO THE GERBER MODEL 48
  - 5.2.1 The `gerber_plot` entity 48
  - 5.2.2 The `image_layer` entity 49
  - 5.2.3 The `interpolation` entity 50
- 5.3 MAPPING FROM THE GERBER MODEL TO THE SVG MODEL 50
  - 5.3.1 Mapping the overlap of the Gerber model and the SVG model 51
  - 5.3.2 Mapping the part of the Gerber model that is not in SVG model's coverage 53
  - 5.3.3 Mapping the implied information in the Gerber model 55
- 5.4 MAPPING IMPLEMENTATION IN JAVA 55
  - 5.4.1 The structure of the Gerber-To-SVG translator 56
  - 5.4.3 Example of jobs done by the Gerber-To-SVG translator 58
- 5.5 CONCLUSIONS 59

CHAPTER 6 WORKED EXAMPLE 2: AGS-TO-SVG TRANSLATOR 60

- 6.1 INTRODUCTION TO THE AGS FORMAT 60
  - 6.1.1 The composition of the AGS Format 60
  - 6.1.2 Groups 62

    6.1.3 The hierarchical structure of the AGS format 62

  6.2 INTRODUCTION TO THE AGS MODEL 63

    6.2.1 Modelling the groups 63

    6.2.2 Modelling the hierarchy structure 64

  6.3 MAPPING FROM THE AGS MODEL TO THE SVG MODEL 64

    6.3.1 Comparing with the mapping between the Gerber model and the SVG model 64

    6.3.2 Mapping issues to be addressed 65

  6.4 THE MAPPING SPECIFICATION IN EMM 67

  6.5 MAPPING IMPLEMENTATION 68

  6.6 CONCLUSIONS 69

REFERENCE 70

APPENDIX 1. SVG_GEOMETRY_MODEL SCHEMA OF THE SVG MODEL 72

APPENDIX 2. SVG_STRUCTURE_MODEL SCHEMA OF THE SVG MODEL 96

Chapter 1 Introduction

The work introduced in this book focuses on knowledge based data translation. Data translation is a task done routinely by a lot of software. Current computer systems are largely file-based, regardless of what operating systems are used. Hence, the communication between systems and components of a system involves file exchange. As there are many different file formats in the current computer world, translating data between different file formats is a common activity.

1.1 Introduction to data translation

Data translation is a problem facing many organizations. A broad spectrum of data is available in distinct heterogeneous sources, stored using different formats. Examples include specific proprietary database vendor formats, the Extended Markup language (XML) [W3Ca] or Latex (Documents) [Latex], Data Exchange (DX) formats (scientific data) and the Standard for the Exchange of Product Model data (STEP) [ISO94a].

Data translation is generally viewed as a task that cannot be generalized or abstracted and hence cannot be automated. Various data formats may be involved in the translation activities. Thus, it makes the translation unpredictable before the concerned data formats are fixed. Different data sources will lead to different translations; different data targets will lead to different translations. Even translation with the same source and target may be different, because of different translation rules. Data translation varies too much to be generalized.

However, automated translator generation, if achievable, could guarantee the quality of translators and speed up translator development. At present, most data translators are generated manually without a general standard and procedure. Automated translator generation will approach the task in a formal way, and the whole procedure could be tested and assessed. Hence, the quality of the generated translators will be improved. The automated approach will leave much of the development process to computers, which ought to be able to do it faster than humans. Therefore, data translators may be developed much faster if automation can be exploited.

Moreover, in a large and complicated software system, many data formats are used and information exchange and data translation are very common. It is difficult to predict all the data formats that are involved or may be involved at some future time. Automated data translator generation can help address this problem and make the systems better able to handle the new data formats that are not included during the initial system development.

1.2 Model based data translation

In this book, a method, which is information model and model mapping based, is offered, trying to address the problem of automated data translation. The main idea is to describe explicitly, in a formal way, the conceptual models of the source and target data formats and the mapping between them. Such models and mappings implicitly occur in the minds of the people who develop data translators manually; the goal here is to emulate that capability.

For example, in Figure 1.1 there are two formats, both of which are used to record circles. In Format-1, a circle is recorded by its centre and diameter, and in Format-2, a circle is recorded by its centre and

```
Format-1
Circle:
Centre: (integer, integer);
```
```
Format-2
Circle:
Centre: (float, float);
```

Figure 1.1 Two Example Formats for Circle

radius. Moreover, in Format-1, all data are integers, whereas all data in Format-2 are floats.

A programmer, who is developing a translator from Format-1 to Format-2, will think of four issues (in Figure 1.2). The first one is that each circle in Format-1 will be translated to a circle in Format-2. The second one is that each centre in Format-1 will be translated to a centre in Format-2. The third one is

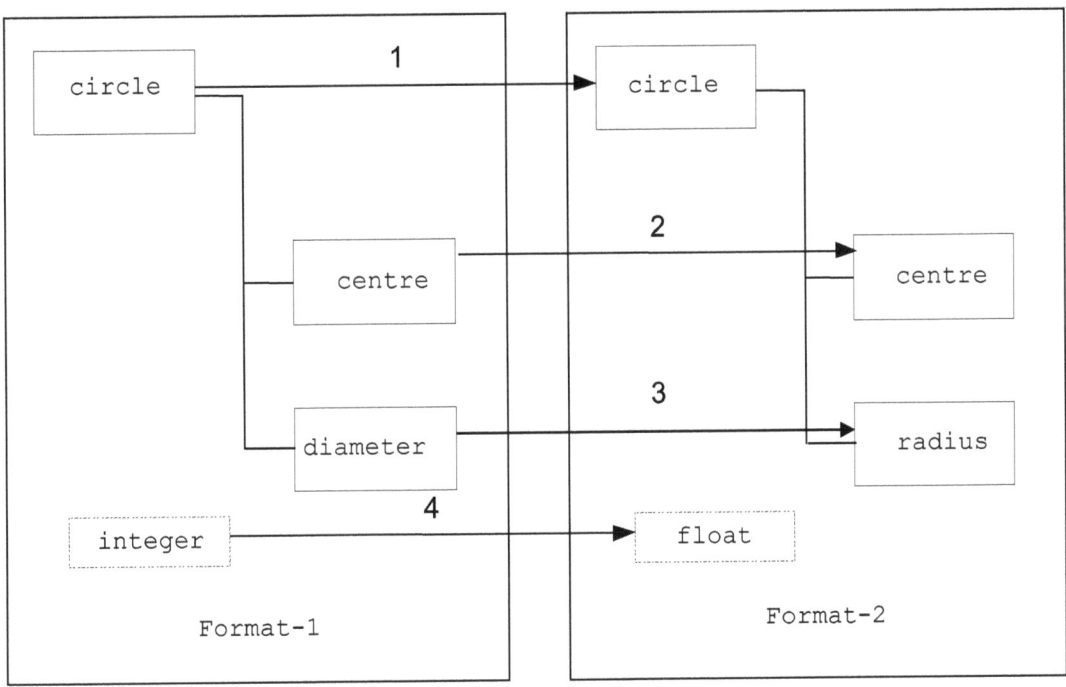

Figure 1.2 Illustration of Translating

that each diameter will be divided by 2 and translated to a radius in Format-2. The fourth one is that all integers in Figure-1 will be transformed to the floats in Format-2. The programmers, who develop the translator manually, inevitably draw out the above ideas and describe them in draft on paper or in their heads informally. Because of the lack of explicit and formal description, both the translation problems and the solutions to them cannot be formally specified and documented. It is difficult to guarantee the quality of the translators that are developed based on informal specification and manual implementation.

Using model based data translation, all the above should be described in a very formal way, which is understandable both to people and to computers. The formal description may improve the specification both of the problems and the solutions and play an important role in the automatic implementation. Then the quality of the translators will be guaranteed in comparison with the ones that are developed based on informal specification and manual implementation.

Information models will be captured to represent the semantics of data formats formally (the contents in Figure 1.1). The translation behaviour (the contents in Figure 1.2) will be described in terms of model mapping, which is the formal description of the relationships between models.

The translators will be generated based on the implementation of the models of the source and the target formats and the mapping between them. Since both of them are interpretable by computers, a software tool can be created to automate the navigation of the information models, map the models under the control of some configuration, interpret and implement the mappings and generate the translator. This is the procedure proposed for eventually creating a model based data translator.

The cores of model-based data translation are the information models of the source and the target data formats and the mapping between these models. The focus of this book is the mapping between the models. The information models of the data formats will be introduced, but are not the focus of this book.

1.3 Model mapping

The mapping activities between models may range from simple to complicate. Some analysis is necessary in order to formally describe the mapping and search for some solutions to address the mapping issues. Its purpose is not to catalogue the mappings, but to show the range and extent of the issues involved.

Some mapping activities may be very simple. These mapping activities only involve simple syntactic changes. The source and the target are in the same domain and hold the same semantics, though their syntaxes are different. The necessary work is only to change the syntactic forms. The example illustrated in Figures 1.1 and 1.2 is a good case in point. The `circles` in `Format-1` and `Format-2` are semantically identical; both describe a circle in the graphical world. The differences between them are at the syntactic level. The `circle` in `Format-1` records the location by its `centre`, and the size by its `diameter`; and all data should be `integers`. The `circle` in `Format-2` records the location by its `centre`, and the size by its `radius`; and all data should be `floats`. Briefly, they are using different structures to hold the same concept. Then the mapping between these `circles` only involves some syntax changes such as transforming the `integer` to `float` and transforming `diameter` to `radius`. `Diameter` and `radius` differ a little semantically, but the differences are so little that a very simple syntactic change can bridge them.

A mapping activity may go across domains. This mapping links models in different domains. A concept in a domain works as the source, which might be mapped to some entities in the other domains. The source and its targets are not semantic equivalents. Such a mapping activity is a view of the source entity from a specific perspective. A source model may be viewed from many angles, so it may be mapped to multiple domains. Figure 1.3 illustrates an example of this case. In the `Economy` domain, there is `money`, and it can be mapped to some concepts in the other domains. `Cheque` and `Travellers' Cheque` in the `Bank` domain, `Bank note` in the `Circulation` domain and `Gold` and `Silver` in the `Metal` domain can do this job. `Money` is a quite abstract concept, and `cheque`, `bank note` and `gold` are its concrete denotations or symbols. In brief, mapping across domains leads a source concept to multiple target concepts each of which describes the source from a specific view.

A mapping activity may be more complicated. This sort of mapping always exists in the mapping specification between complex models. The source and the target models depict a system from different views, and neither of them covers the whole system although they may have some overlap. Moreover,

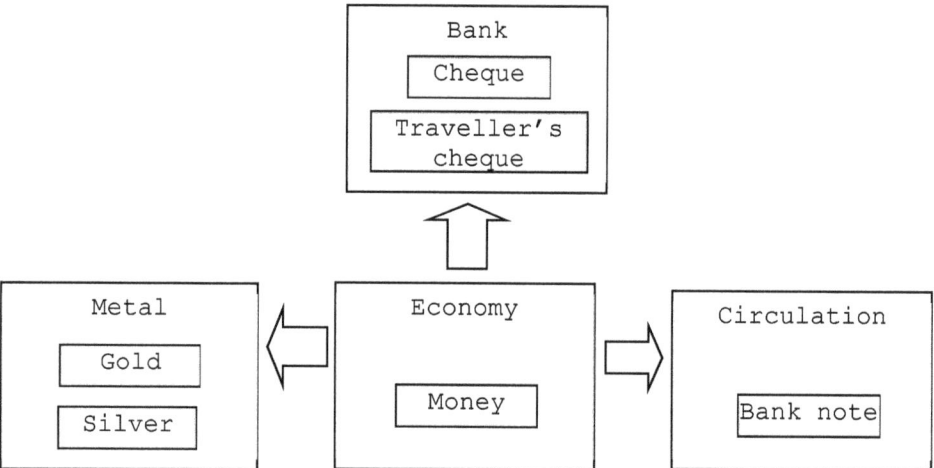

Figure 1.3 Illustration of Cross-domain Mapping

the information to be mapped is implied in the source model, not explicitly identified. Generating or updating the target information requires analysis and integration of the information obtained from the source model. In the Unified Modelling Language (UML) [Rational97] family, there are the use-case specification and the class diagram (in Figure 1.4). The mapping between them is a good case in point. When designing a system, both the use-case and the class diagram perform some useful functions. A use-case diagram describes the functionality the system should deliver, as perceived by external actors, whereas a class diagram shows the static structure of classes in the system. Theoretically, it is possible to draw a class diagram from the use-case specification. However, there is no explicitly defined information that is about class diagrams in the use-case specification. Attempting this form of mapping will lead to parsing and analysis of both the use-case and the class diagram specifications.

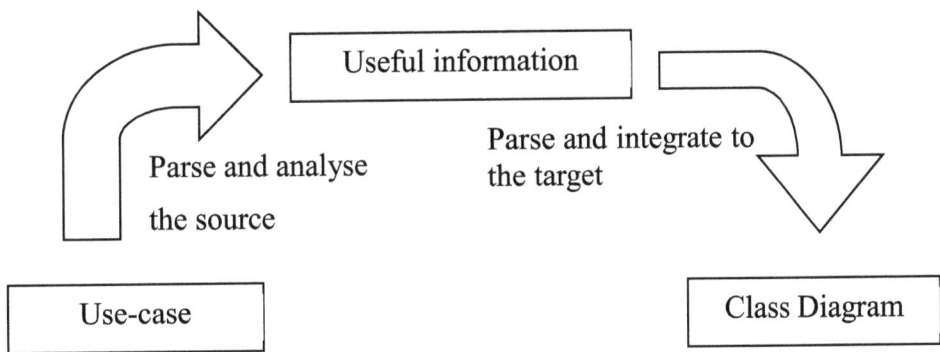

Figure 1.4 Illustration of Complicated Mapping

1.4 Contents of the book

This book is a description of the information models and the mapping between models that have been studied in order to gain a better understanding of the rules involved in automated data translation. An information model (the model of Scalable Vector Graphics (SVG) [W3Cb]) was created, and has been used as the target of experimental mapping from two different models; one is the Gerber [Gerber91] model and the other is the Association of Geotechnical and Geoenvironmental Specialists (AGS) [AGS99] model. Two worked examples (the Gerber-to-SVG and the AGS-to-SVG translators) were produced manually based on the above mapping specifications for the purposes of testing and evaluating the model based approach.

The models of the data formats that are the source and the target of the translator are in the EXPRESS language [ISO94b]. Then experimental mappings from the source model to the target model were created and described based on the EXPRESS Model Mapping (EMM). EMM originated from the worked examples in Chapter 5 and 6, and is a draft at the time of writing of this book. The study of EMM will continue in future work. EMM is not intended to take the place of existing mapping languages such as EXPRESS-X [ISO99], but works as a mapping specification method. The relationship between EMM and the model mapping languages is similar to the relationship between pseudo code and programming languages.

There are seven chapters in this book. This is the first one. Chapter 2 describes information models, Chapter 3 describes the mapping between models, Chapter 4 describes the SVG model, Chapter 5 is the introduction to the Gerber-to-SVG translator, which is a worked example, Chapter 6 is about another worked example, the AGS-to-SVG translator.

Chapter 2 Information modelling and the use of EXPRESS

The purpose of this chapter is to introduce information modelling, which is the basic technology in the context of this book.

Some information modelling technologies such as the Universal Modelling Language (UML), the Integrated Computer-Aided Manufacturing (ICAM) Definition (IDEF) [IDEF98] and EXPRESS (including the EXPRESS language and the EXPRESS-G [ISO94b] graphical representation) are introduced and illustrated with some examples. The focus, however, is on EXPRESS, which was selected for all the information models in this book.

2.1 Information models

An information model is a formal description of an area of interest (a domain). It specifies the objects within the domain, the relationships between the objects, the basic attributes of the objects and the constraints upon the objects and their relationships [Mint]. Its purpose is to identify clearly the objects in a particular "Universe of Discourse". An information model allows people to communicate more accurately about a domain of common interest.

An information model is a formal specification that is understandable not only to people but also to computers. Hence, software tools can process it for some further purpose such as automated code generation or software simulation.

In the following section, the modelling features that are required to construct information models are presented. This description is followed by an overview of some of the commonly used information model representations.

2.2 The features of an information model

An information model should be a conceptual description which does not contain implementation specific details. This allows the information modeller to concentrate on the structure and semantics of the information, without also having to think about how it is going to be implemented. An information model describes the static structure of objects and how they are related. It does not describe their dynamic behaviour. For example, it does not show how the objects interact with each other, or how they vary over time.

In the following sections, the most important and widely accepted features that are required to describe information models are introduced. In the description, it is sometimes helpful to think about how an information model might be instantiated.

2.2.1 Objects

An important information modelling requirement is the ability to represent the objects of interest in the domain being modelled.

An object, in the context of software engineering, can only be created dynamically following a previously defined class. Hence, an object is an instance of a specified class; the types of its characteristics or attributes are declared in its class before its instantiation. For example, in an object-oriented programming language such as C++ or Java, before creating an object, the class to which it belongs should be defined.

This holds too for information models. An information model statically describes a domain of interest. It does not focus on a single object or instance but on an abstraction of a category of objects with some common characteristics. In other words, an information model does not define or create single objects, but focuses on the definition and abstraction of all possible objects in the domain and their categorization. A category of objects is often called an entity in information modelling languages.

Club Member				
Name	**ID No.**	**Gender**	Address	Membership Type
John Smith	0011239	Male	60 Pine Road	Gold
Yuki Lee	0011240	Female	3B Bigstone Building	Silver
Andrew Clark	0011241	Male	Flat 5 Fleet Garden	Silver

Table 2.1 Example of Club Member Information

There are three members of a club listed in Table 2.1. In the context of software engineering, they can be recognized as three objects, each of which has some characteristics such as a name, an ID number, a gender specification, an address and a membership type. However, an information model of this table does not focus on the different attribute values of these three members, such as John Smith's ID No and Yuki Lee's address, but on the abstraction of the information of all members. One entity, `club_member`, will be created to represent all members, and all specified members will be instances of it. Other entities, `club_member_gold` and `club_member_silver`, will be created too. They can represent the member status differences.

An entity should encapsulate all the information that is relevant to its target concept in the real world. It should also have an identifying name, which allows people who read the model to make a mental association between the model and its target in the real world.

2.2.2 Attributes

In an information model, an entity may have one or more attributes. The attributes describe the characteristics of the concept represented by the entity. Attributes are optional; an entity is valid without any attributes. An attribute should have a name that identifies the attributes and provides meaning to the reader.

The `club_member` entity that captures the information about the club members in Table 2.1 should have four attributes: `name`, `ID_number`, `gender` and `address`. The `membership_type` could be captured as a generalization/specialization relationship between the `club_member` entity and the `club_member_gold` and the `club_member_silver` entities, see section 2.23.

Entities should only include the attributes that are relevant to the intended focus of the model. There are potentially an unlimited number of attributes that could be assigned to some entities. However, adding more attributes than is necessary will result in a large model whose important concepts are less clear. For example, the `club_member` entity may have some extra attributes such as `hair_colour` and `favourite_popgroup`, which are not necessary when considering the membership of a club, unless it is a pop music club. Including non-relevant attributes may affect the semantic clarity of the model and could lead to unnecessary work in any future implementation that conforms to the model.

2.2.3 Relationships between objects

There are two sorts of relationships between the entities of an information model: generalization/specialization relationship and association relationship.

The `club_member` entity is general, whereas the `club_member_gold` and the `club_member_silver` entities are more specific in terms of membership status. The generalization/specialization is created and maintained by the inheritance mechanism of the information modelling method.

Associations represent relationships between instances of entities. Associations typically include cardinality. It should also be possible to specify whether an ordering is required on the relationship.

Club Profile	
Club Name	Good Citizens Association
Club Address	113 Mary Street
Club Telephone Number	0161 222 8965
Club members	See the table of club member information

Table 2.2 Example of Club Profile

A `club_profile` entity can be made to capture the information shown in Table 2.2, which has four attributes: `club_name`, `club_address`, `club_telephone_number` and `club_members`. The `club_profile` entity has a relationship to the `club_member` entity. One of the `club_profile` entity's attributes, `club_members`, will refer to the `club_member` entity. This relationship will be specified with a one-to-many cardinality, because a club can contain many members and must have at least one member. Section 2.4.1 and 2.4.2 use this example to illustrate alternative modelling approaches using UML and IDEF1X.

2.2.4 Constraints on objects and their relationships

It should be possible to add constraints to an information model. A constraint is a rule that specifies further restrictions on the model. An instance of the information model must conform to all constraints in order to be valid. There are a number of different cases where constraints would be useful. This includes constraints that affect the attributes of an object, and constraints on the relationships between objects.

A reasonable constraint on the `club_profile` entity may be that the number of members must be more than one.

2.3 What an information model is not

An information model is not a data model, even though terms such as schema are used for both information models and data models. A data model focuses on the implementation, not on the conceptual design. It often reflects an implementation strategy, and is used in database management system design. Compared with a data model, an information model focuses on describing the semantics of the information and the relationships between information items. It does not focus on the implementation of the design.

An information model is also not a program. It cannot be compiled and executed directly.

2.4 Ways of describing an information model

An information model may be described textually and diagrammatically. The textual approach includes the Z method [ZN] and the EXPRESS language. The diagrammatic approach includes Integrated Definition for Information Modelling (IDEF1X) [IDEF98], EXPRESS-G and UML.

In the following sections, UML and IDEF1X are briefly introduced. The EXPRESS language and the EXPRESS-G representation will be introduced in detail in Sections 2.5 and 2.6.

2.4.1 UML

UML was developed in order to unify the concepts of a number of existing object-oriented analysis and design methods. These include Booch [Booch94], OMT [Rumb91] and OOSE [Jacobson92]. The language was initiated by Rational Software Corp, but is now contributed to by a consortium Object Management Group (OMG) [OMG].

The UML language consists of a number of different diagram notations that share some common conventions. These notations include static diagrams, use-case diagrams, sequence diagrams, state diagrams and activity diagrams. The UML language provides a rich set of mechanisms to roughly describe a system's usage scenarios, classes and objects involved, state changes during transactions and operation sequencing. This section is restricted to describing the static structure diagrams, which involve the class diagrams only. The methods of the class diagrams are out of consideration too, because they are not in the domain of the static structure.

The example of club members (Table 2.1) and club profile (Table 2.2) in UML class diagram form is shown in Figure 2.1. In UML, a class represents the modelling concept of an entity. It is depicted by a rectangle, which can be divided into parts by using horizontal lines. The top part contains the class name. The next part contains a list of attributes, where each attribute is an identifier followed by a data type. A third part contains a list of operations. The attributes and operations of a class are optional. In Figure 2.1, there are four classes: club_profile, club_member, club_member_gold and club_member_silver. The short dash "-" symbols before the attributes specify that the attributes' accessibility is private. The accessibility specification is not necessary to the information models. However, it is mandatory in the UML class diagrams.

In UML, an association is shown as a line that connects two class symbols. Some information about the cardinality, ordering (if the cardinality is greater than zero) and role names can be added to the association symbols. In Figure 2.1, an association connects the club_profile and the club_member classes. The club_profile class plays a role of owner, and it can own one or more than one instances of the club_member class. The club_member class plays a role of owned_by, and it must be owned by one and only one instance of the club_profile class.

The generalization/specification is described by the inheritance in UML. It is shown as a line from the more specific classes to a more general class. A hollow triangle is used to indicate the direction. In Figure 2.1, the club_member_gold class and the club_member_silver class are two more specific subclasses to the club_member class. The name of the club_member class is in italics because it is abstract, which means it is not instantiatable.

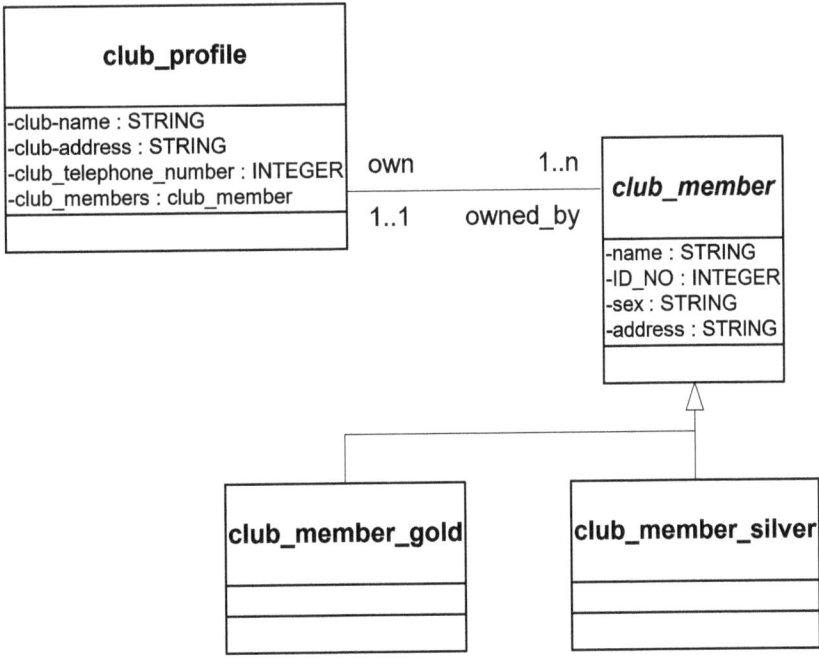

Figure 2.1 Club Example Described in the UML Class Diagram

2.4.2 IDEF1X

The Integrated Computer-Aided Manufacturing (ICAM) Definition (IDEF) set of methods has been developed to perform modelling in support of enterprise integration. There are a number of different methods in IDEF, where each method has a different modelling role. Within the IDEF family, IDEF1 is available for information modelling. IDEF1 was extended to form the Integration Definition for Information Modelling (IDEF1X). IDEF1X is more commonly used than IDEF1. The IDEF1X method is intended primarily as a method for designing relational databases, although it can be used for other tasks. For example, it requires that entities are distinguished by keys. This is a requirement for relational databases, but not for information modelling.

The IDEF1X method makes use of the concepts of entity, attribute and relationship. Figure 2.2 shows the IDEF1X representation of the example of club member (Table 2.1) and club profile (Table 2.2). Entities are represented by boxes. The name of the entity is above the box. The attributes are inside the box. The attributes that are above the horizontal line of a box form the primary key of the entity. A primary key uniquely identifies an instance of the entity. In Figure 2.2, there are four entities: `club_profile`, `club_member`, `club_member_gold` and `club_member_silver`. The primary keys are not necessary in the context of information modelling. Presumably, the `club_name` attribute is set to be the primary key of the `club_profile` entity, and the `ID_No` attribute to be the one of the `club_member` entity.

In IDEF1X, an association is depicted by a line that joins exactly two entities. This is shown in Figure 2.2 for the `have_members` relationship. The association starts from the non-dotted side to the dotted (●) side.

IDEF1X can represent the generalization/specialization relationship by a circle with two lines underneath. In Figure 2.2, the `club_member` entity is the generalization of the `club_member_gold` and `club_member_silver` entities.

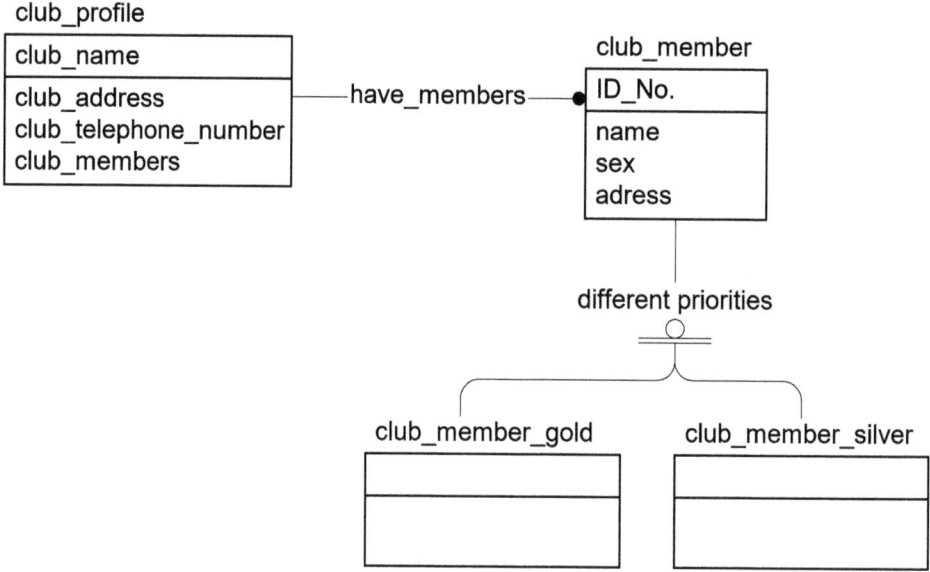

Figure 2.2 Club Example Described in IDEF1X

2.5 The EXPRESS language and its EXPRESS-G graphical representation

The EXPRESS language is an international standard (ISO 10303-11). It is a formal information model specification language.

The EXPRESS language is readable to humans and fully computer interpretable. It was originally developed within the context of STEP, but is currently used for many other purposes, including applications outside STEP.

EXPRESS-G provides a graphical notation for a subset of the EXPRESS language constructs. It is intended for human communication. In the following introduction to EXPRESS, the corresponding EXPRESS-G symbols will be presented too.

In this section, an example will be used to illustrate schemas, entities, attributes, and generalization/specialization relationships in EXPRESS. This example model is the point concept in the geometrical domain. A `point` has an `x-coordinate`, a `y-coordinate` and an optional `z-coordinate`. A `coordinate` can be relative or absolute, and it has a coordinate value attribute, to which a `length` entity can be referenced. This particular notation is taken from the world of the SVG format where a coordinate value is a length. A length can be specified using three units: metres, centimetres and millimetres, with millimetres as the default. The example model will be described in both the textual form of EXPRESS and the EXPRESS-G graphical form (See Figure 2.4). The detail of the EXPRESS language and the corresponding symbols in EXPRESS-G are introduced in the following sections.

```
SCHEMA pointModel;
TYPE value = REAL;
WHERE
    notLessThanZero : SELF >= 0.0;
END_TYPE;
ENTITY point;
x: coordinate;
    y: coordinate;
    z: OPTIONAL coordinate;
END_ENTITY;
ENTITY coordinate;
    ABSTRACT SUPERTYPE OF (ONEOF (absoluteCoordinate,
                                  relativeCoordinate) );
    coordinateValue : length;
INVERSE
    containingPointX : SET [0:1] OF point FOR x;
    containingPoinyY : SET [0:1] OF point FOR y;
    containingPointZ : SET [0:1] OF point FOR z;
containingRelativeCoordinate : SET [0:1] OF relativeCoordinate FOR lastCoordinate;
WHERE
    validExistence :SIZEOF(containingPointX)+
              SIZEOF(containingPointY)+
                  SIZEOF(containingPointZ)+
       SIZEOF(containingRelativeCoordinate)    = 1;
END_ENTITY;
ENTITY absoluteCoordinate;
    SUBTYPE OF (coordinate);
END_ENTITY;
ENTITY relativeCoordinate;
    SUBTYPE OF (coordinate);
    lastCoordinate : coordinate;
```

```
END_ENTITY;
ENTITY length
    ABSTRACT SUPERTYPE OF(ONEOF (lengthInMetre,
                    lengthInCentimetre,
                        lengthInMillimetre));
    lengthValueInMillimetre : value;
INVERSE
containingCoordinate : coordinate FOR coordinateValue;
END_ENTITY;
ENTITY lengthInMetre
    SUBTYPE OF(length);
    lengthValueInMetre : value;
DERIVE
    SELF\length.lengthValueInMillimetre : value := lengthValueInMetre*1000;
END_ENTITY;
ENTITY lengthInCentimetre
    SUBTYPE OF(length);
    lengthValueInCentimetre : value;
DERIVE
    SELF\length.lengthValueInMillimetre : value := lengthValueInCentimetre*10;
END_ENTITY;
ENTITY lengthInMillimetre
    SUBTYPE OF(length);
END_ENTITY;
END_SCHEMA;
```

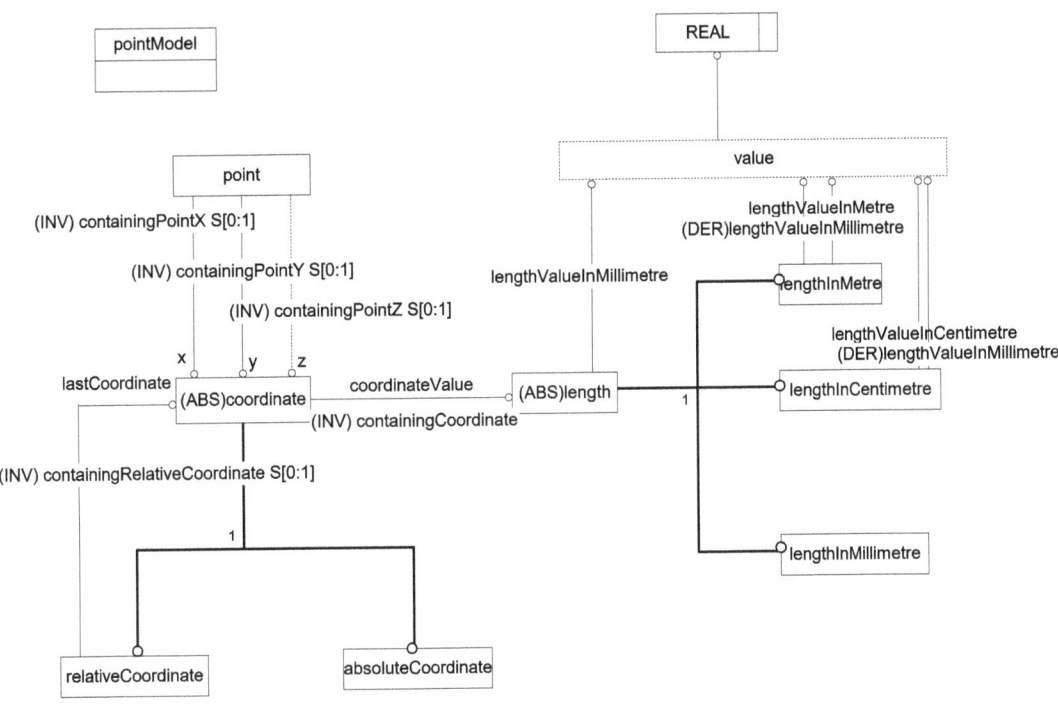

Figure 2.3 the `PointModel` schema in EXPRESS-G

2.5.1 SCHEMA

In EXPRESS, a schema is a wrapper for a collection of related information. It is used to encompass the objects, relationships and constraints for a particular universe of functionality. In other words, the contents in a given schema must all describe a common domain. A schema is defined by a pair of tags, the head one is SCHEMA, followed by identification, and the tail one is END_SCHEMA. Between them is the schema body, which consists of some declarations. In the above example, there is one schema, `pointModel`. In Figure 2.3, the `pointModel` schema in EXPRESS-G is described by a rectangle with the identification enclosed in it. The identification is above a horizontal line that is in the centre of the rectangle.

The order in which objects are declared is not relevant to the meaning of a schema as a whole or to the individual things declared within it. There must be well-defined limits to a given schema. It cannot describe everything, but should be constrained to fit the domain intended. A single schema cannot sensibly be used to describe two or more different domains.

An EXPRESS information model may include one or more schemas, but the schema definitions may not be nested. A schema can draw from declarations made in other schemas. There are two interface specifications (USE and REFERENCE), both of which enable item visibility. The USE specification allows items declared in one schema to be independently instantiated in the schema specifying the USE construct, whereas the items that are explicitly referenced by a REFERENCE construct shall only be instantiated to play the role described by an attribute of an instantiation of an entity in the schema.

2.5.2 Data types

This section introduces the data types provided as part of the EXPRESS language. Every attribute, local variable or formal parameter has an associated data type. The data types in EXPRESS can be classified as simple data types, aggregation data types, named data types, constructed data types and generalized data types. They are shown in Figure 2.4.

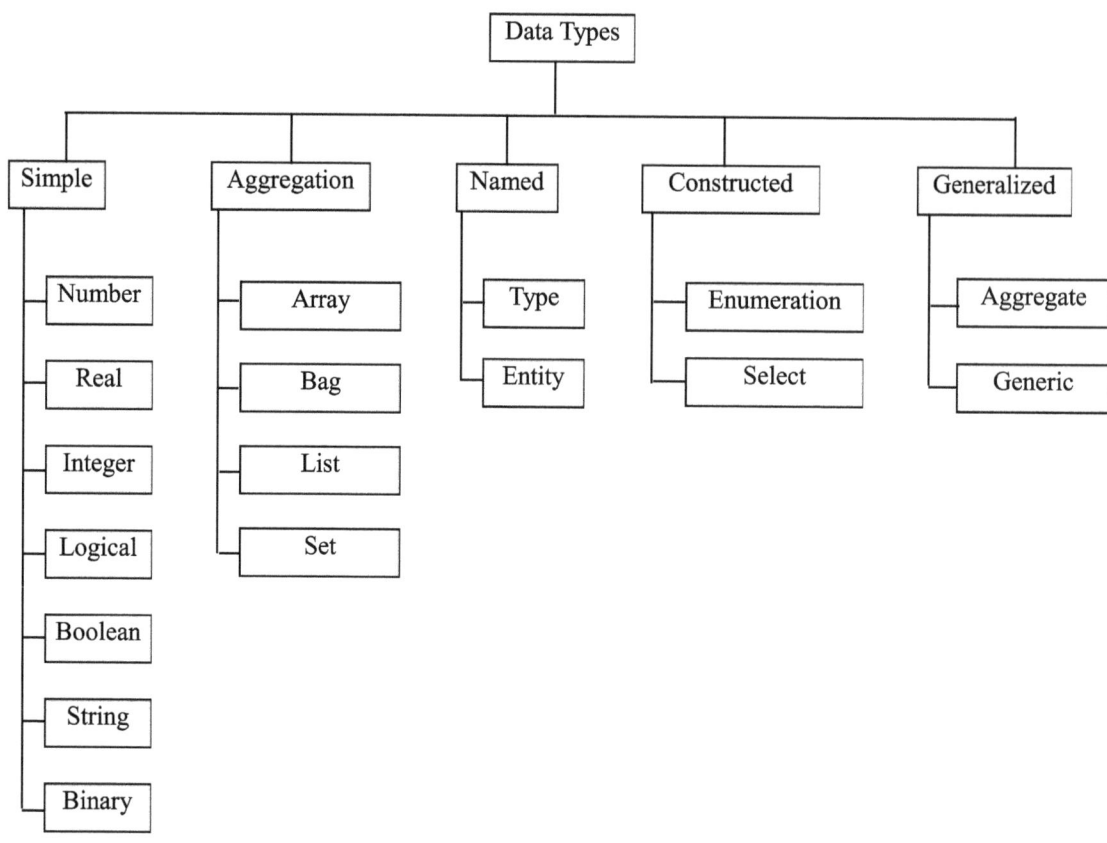

Figure 2.4 Data Types in EXPRESS

2.5.2.1 Simple data type

The simple data types define the domain of the atomic units in EXPRESS. That is they cannot be further subdivided into elements that EXPRESS recognizes. The simple data types are NUMBER, REAL, BINARY, INTEGER, LOGICAL, BOOLEAN and STRING [ISO94b]. Figure 2.5 illustrates the symbols used for simple data types in EXPRESS-G. A simple data type is denoted by a rectangular solid box with a double vertical line at the right end of the box. The name of the data type is enclosed within the box.

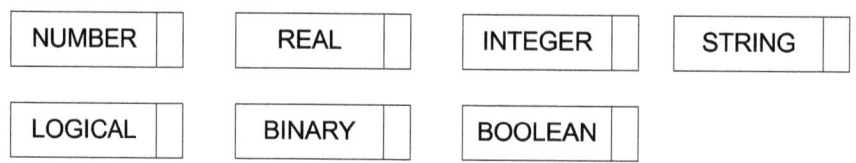

Figure 2.5 Basic Data Types in EXPRESS-G

In Figure 2.3, the REAL simple data type is used to define the value named data type.

2.5.2.2 Aggregation data type

Aggregation data types have as their domain collections of values of a given base data type. These base data type values are called elements of the aggregation collection. There are four kinds of aggregation data type: BAG, SET, LIST and ARRAY. Each kind of aggregation data type attaches different properties to its values [ISO94b]. The four sorts of aggregation data type differ in three aspects: the size specification variability, the indexing/ordering of elements and element occurrence. This is shown in Table 2.3.

The declaration of an aggregation data type consists of aggregation data identification, an optional boundary specification and base type identification. In the pointModel schema, all the INVERSE attributes of the coordinate entity are assigned SET aggregation data type.

Aggregation Type	Size	Index/order	Element occurrence
ARRAY	Fixed	Indexed	Multiple/unique
LIST	Variable	Ordered	Multiple/unique
SET	Variable	Unordered	Unique
BAG	Variable	Unordered	Multiple

Table 2.3 Aggregation Data Types in EXPRESS

2.5.2.3 Named data type

The named data types are the data types that may be declared in a formal specification. There are two kinds of data type: the `entity` data type and the defined data types.

`Entity` data types are established by entity declarations. The `entity` data type is introduced in Section 2.5.3.

A defined data type is created based on another type (the underlying type). The `value` data type in the `pointModel` schema is an example of a defined data type; it is created based on the `REAL` simple data type. The semantics of a defined data type is greater than its underlying type. A defined data type can be used to distinguish conceptually different collections of values that happen to have similar representations. With the help of defined data types, the maintainability of the model is increased.

In EXPRESS, a named data type is defined by a pair of tags. The head tag is `TYPE,` followed by identification and the underlying data type. The tail tag is `END_TYPE`. In EXPRESS-G, the symbol for a named data type consists of a dashed box enclosing its name. In Figure 2.3, the `value` named data type is a good case in point.

2.5.2.4 Constructed data type

There are two kinds of constructed data types in EXPRESS: `ENUMERATION` data types and `SELECT` data types, described in Table 2.4. These data types have similar syntactic structures and are used to provide the underlying representation of defined data types.

Constructed data type	Description
`ENUMERATION` data type	It defines an ordered set of names. It is used to make data available as a set of static values.
`SELECT` data type	It makes defined data types available as a grouped set of named data types.

Table 2.4 Constructed Data Types in EXPRESS

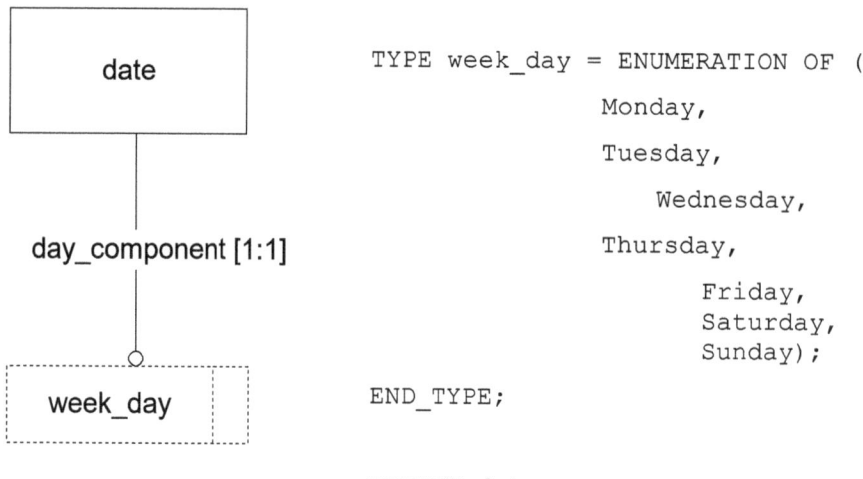

Figure 2.6 The Week_day Enumeration Data Type in EXPRESS-G and EXPRESS

In EXPRESS, a constructed data type is defined by a pair of tags. The head tag is TYPE, followed by its identification and the constructed data type, ENUMERATION or SELECT. The tail tag is END_TYPE. Between them is a list of the basic elements. In EXPRESS-G, the symbol for a constructed data type consists of a dashed box enclosing its name, with double lines at one end. The ENUMERATION has the double lines at the right end, whereas the SELECT has the double lines at the left end. Figure 2.6 is an example of the ENUMERATION data type. The week_day is an enumeration of all weekdays, and the day_component attribute of the date entity receives values of this ENUMERATION data type.

2.5.2.5 Generalized data type

The generalized data types are used to specify a generalization of other data types, and can only be used in certain contexts. The GENERIC type is a generalization of all data types. The AGGREGATE data type is a generalization of all aggregation data types. Both of them can only be used as the types of the formal parameters of functions and procedures.

```
FUNCTION scale (in:AGGREGATE OF INTEGER, scalar:NUMBER) : AGGREGATE OF INTEGER;

LOCAL
    Result:AGGREGATE OF INTEGER := [];
END_LOCAL;

REPEAT i:= LOINDEX(in) TO HIINDEX(in);
    Result[i] := scalar *in[i];
END_REPEAT;

RETURN (result);

END_FUNCTION;
```

There is a scale function in the above excerpt of an information model in EXPRESS. The data type of the in formal parameter is AGGREGATE, which means the actual parameter can be a BAG, SET, ARRAY or LIST.

2.5.3 ENTITY

An entity represents an object of interest in the universe of discourse. In other words, it is a class of information, which represents conceptual or real world objects that have common properties. In the pointModel example, there are eight entities: point, coordinate, absoluteCoordinate, length, lengthInMetre, lengthInCentimetre and lengthInMillimetre.

An entity can also play the role of a data type. In the pointModel schema in Figure 2.3, the length

15

entity is the data type of the values that the `coordinateValue` attribute of the `coordinate` entity may receive. On the other hand, the `length` entity holds some semantics dependently and means more than a data type; it means the length in that model. Therefore, an entity represents a real world object, which may work as a data type too.

In EXPRESS, an entity is declared by a pair of tags; the head tag is `ENTITY`, followed by identification, the tail tag is `END_TAG`. Between them is the body of the `entity`, which consists of some `attributes` and `constraints`.

EXPRESS-G uses the solid box symbol for `ENTITY` definition. The name of the entity is enclosed by the box. In Figure 2.3, the `point` entity is an example.

2.5.4 Attributes

An attribute is a characteristic, quality or property of an entity. It can be qualified by various additional specifiers, such as `OPTIONAL`, `UNIQUE`, `DERIVE` and `INVERSE`.

It is not always necessary to specify values for all attributes defined in an entity. Where it is not always assigned a value, an attribute may be marked as `OPTIONAL`. An optional attribute that happens not to have an explicitly assigned value is given the value indeterminate (?). For example, the z attribute of the `point` entity (See Figure 2.3) is not mandatory, because the z-coordinate is not mandatory for a 2D point. Therefore, the z attribute is marked `OPTIONAL`.

The `UNIQUE` keyword is used in two different contexts. The first context is that `UNIQUE` can be associated with an aggregation attribute definition. For example, a list of member of a group might be defined as:

`group_members : LIST [0:?] OF UNIQUE member;`

In this statement, `UNIQUE` means that all members of the `LIST` must be different from each other.

The `UNIQUE` keyword can also be used to specify a form of rule that applies to all occurrences of the current entity type in a representation of the Universe of Discourse.

An attribute declared in a supertype can be redeclared in its subtypes. In the `2D-point` example, the `lengthValueInMillimetre` of supertype `length` is redeclared in its subtypes `lengthInmetre` and `lengthInCentimetre`, because it should be calculated from the other private attributes of the subtypes.

The use of `INVERSE` makes the attribute dependency relationship explicit for certain cases. It is used, in the context of this book, to specify existence dependency between an entity and the use of that entity. For example, the `point` entity uses `coordinate` entity to define the data types of its attributes such as x and y, so the existence of the `coordinate` entity is dependent on the `point` entity.

In EXPRESS-G, an attribute of an entity is described by a line between the entity and the data types of the values of the attribute. On the line end that connects the symbol of the data types of the values, there is a little circle. The identification and some other specifiers of the attribute are placed on the line.

2.5.5 Generalization/specialization

The EXPRESS language uses a `supertype/subtype` mechanism to represent the generalization/specialization relationship.

A `subtype` entity is more specific than its `supertypes`, and a `supertype` entity is more general than its `subtypes`. A `subtype` entity inherits all of the properties of its `supertypes`, including attributes and constraints. For example, the `coordinate` entity is a `supertype` and has two `subtypes`, `absoluteCoordinate` and `relativeCoordinate`. Coordinates are general and can be classified to be absolute coordinates or relative ones. The `coordinateValue` attribute will be inherited by the `subtypes`.

A `subtype` entity may have more than one `supertype`, so the EXPRESS language supports multiple-inheritance.

A `supertype` entity may be abstract, which means it is not instantiatable.

In EXPRESS-G, the entities forming an inheritance graph are connected by thick solid lines. The circled end of the relationship line denotes the subtype end of the relationship. When a `supertype` is ABSTRACT, the characters ABS, enclosed by parentheses, precede the name of the entity within the entity symbol box.

2.6 Conclusions

This chapter defines and describes information modelling. Various model representations are introduced, but the focus is on the EXPRESS language that is the modelling language used in the context of this book.

The UML class diagram, IDEF1X, EXPRESS and EXPRESS-G can all specify information models. UML is expressive because of its graphical presentation, most types its diagram are also behaviour oriented. The class diagram of UML is quite generic; extensions of it are available to meet some specified modelling methods, but the constraints cannot be formally defined.. EXPRESS is a textual form modelling method, and constraints can be formally defined, and EXPRESS-G is the graphical form of it. EXPRESS-G is more expressive than the EXPRESS language, but it cannot formally represent the constraints. IDEF1X, like EXPRESS-G as a graphical language, is expressive, but its ability to specify constraints is more limited than is typical for textual information modelling languages such as EXPRESS. Another disadvantage is that it is targeted towards a relational database implementation, rather than being generic.

In Chapter 3 mapping between information models will be introduced. Information models and model mapping are the two core methods proposed for addressing the data translation problem.

Chapter 3 Information model mapping

After the introduction to information models and EXPRESS in Chapter 2, this chapter focuses on the mapping between models.

Data translations are implemented in the main based on mapping between models of the data formats being used. The capability and quality of the data translators are dependent on the model mappings.

The contents and targets of an information model mapping will be described in this chapter. Some EXPRESS model mapping languages such as EXPRESS-X [ISO99], EXPRESS-V [Hardwick94] and EXPRESS-M [EM95] will be introduced.

A general EXPRESS model mapping representation, EXPRESS Model Mapping (EMM) will also be described and illustrated by some examples. It originated from the worked examples that will be introduced in Chapter 5 and 6. EMM focuses on semantics during mapping, while the mapping languages concentrate more on data. EMM describes the mapping in a general way, not bound to a specified mapping language.

3.1 Information Model Mapping

Mapping between models means conveying information in the source schema to the target schema and representing it in an appropriate manner. An information model describes the static structure of objects in a domain of interest and the relationships between the entities such as inheritance and composition. It does not describe their dynamic behaviours, such as the interaction with other models at run time, though the modelling languages in which it is specified may be capable of defining dynamic activities. Mapping is an activity that links the source and the target models, and describes the way in which the instances of the target model are generated and updated according to the instances of the source model.

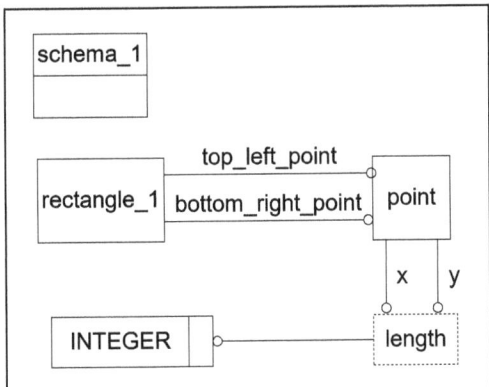 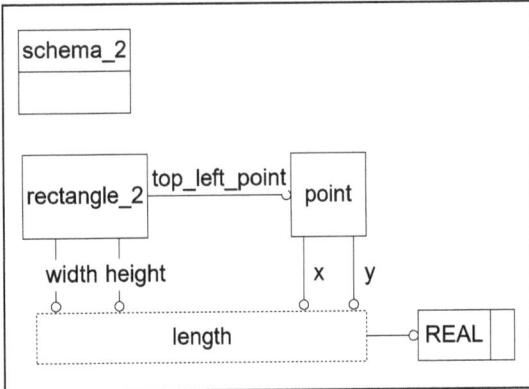

Figure 3.1 Two Models of Rectangle

In Figure 3.1, there are two schemas: `schema_1` and `schema_2`. Below is the description of the models in the EXPRESS language.

```
SCHEMA schema_1;
ENTITY rectangle_1;
    top_left_point      : point;
    bottom_right_point  : point;
END_ENTITY;
```

```
ENTITY point;
    x : length;
    y : length;
END_ENTITY;
TYPE length = INTEGER;
END_TYPE;
END_SCHEMA;


SCHEMA schema_2;
ENTITY rectangle_2;
    top_left_point : point;
    width : length;
    height : length;
END_ENTITY;
ENTITY point;
    x : length;
    y : length;
END_ENTITY;
TYPE length = REAL;
END_TYPE;
END_SCHEMA;
```

From the names of the entities and attributes in Figure 3.1, both schemas capture the geometrical concept of rectangle. In `schema_1`, a `rectangle_1` entity has two attributes `top_left_point` and `bottom_right_point`. In `schema_2`, a `rectangle_2` entity has three attributes `topLeftPoint`, `width` and `height`. The mapping from the `rectangle_1` entity in the `schema_1` schema to the `rectangle_2` entity in the `schema_2` schema should describe a process such that the `top_left_point` attribute of the `rectangle_2` entity should be equal to the `top_left_point` attribute of the `rectangle_1` entity; the `width` attribute of the `rectangle_2` entity should be equal to the difference between the `x` attributes of the `point` entities that are assigned to the `bottom_right_point` attribute and to the `top_left_point` attribute of `rectangle_1`; the `height` attribute of the `rectangle_2` entity should be equal to the difference between the `y` attributes of the `point` entities that are assigned to the `bottom_right_point` attribute and to the `top_left_point` attribute of `rectangle_1`. In order to finish the mapping between `rectangle_1` and `rectangle_2`, some other mapping specification about the `point` entities and `length` data type are necessary too.

Another mapping, which is from `rectangle_2` to `rectangle_1`, can also be described in the similar way. The mapping is not commutative.

A mapping between two information models is essentially a set of rules, which define how to generate the data instances of the target model from the information derived from the data instances of the source model.

3.2 Requirements on model mappings

From the mathematical point of view, a mapping is defined by its source, target and mapping rules. Here source is the domain from which information is drawn out; target means the domain to which information is conveyed and in which it is represented; and the mapping rules are the mathematical specification of relationships between the source and the target.

All these three aspects are very important and the keys to a mapping. Concentration is always put on the mapping rules. Different mapping rules certainly lead to different mappings. However, the specifications of the mapping source and target are also very important. Therefore, the mapping specification should be able to define the source, the target and the mapping rules.

3.3 Information model mapping languages

The mapping between EXPRESS information models can be formally depicted in various approaches such as the EXPRESS-X language. These mapping languages have been developed in the context of STEP.

In 1992, a simple language-based toolkit that could be used to migrate ISO 10303-21 files was developed. The system was called TransformR [Clark92]. It has an elegant style and appears well suited to the process of propagating data between versions of the same schema. TransformR is, however, very much a unidirectional mapping language, with limited functionality in terms of the combinations of entities that can be clustered and created. It is also limited in the types of equivalences that can be specified between attributes [Amor97]. For example, TransformR cannot convert an aggregate value from one (`array`, `bag`, `list` or `set`) into another, and it cannot apply any constraints such as WHERE rules to the data migration either.

The next language to be published was EXPRESS-M, which took some of the concepts of TransformR and built upon these to produce a full-blown mapping language that could be used for complex conversions of large amount of data. EXPRESS-M is a schema mapping language, which means that it is used to describe how entity instances should be mapped between schemas in order to facilitate the transfer of data between models described by those schemas. Table 3.1 illustrates the main components of EXPRESS-M.

EXPRESS-M components	Description
SCHEMA_MAP	It specifies the EXPRESS schemas that are the source for the mapping and the schemas that are the target for the mapping.
MAP	It specifies the mapping between entities in the source schema(s) and the entities in the target schema(s).
TYPE_MAP	It specifies the mapping required to instantiate an attribute of one type from an attribute of a second type.
PRUNE	It specifies entities that might be created twice in a SCHEMA_MAP and which should be culled to one instance.

Table 3.1 The Major Components of EXPRESS-M

EXPRESS-V appeared shortly after EXPRESS-M, and took a different approach to the mapping process. The language was based around Structure Query Language (SQL) [SRP] and intended to produce updateable views of EXPRESS defined data. Table 3.2 illustrates the major components of EXPRESS-V.

EXPRESS-V components	Description
VIEW	It specifies that an entity or entities are to be viewed as another entity.
VIEW_ASSIGN	It specifies what attributes in the target schema need to be updated when source entities are modified.
UPDATE	It specifies what attributes in the source schema need to be updated when target entities are modified.
CREATE	It specifies attributes values for source entities that have to be created by the creation of target entities.
DELETE	It specifies which attributes and objects need to be deleted in the source entities

	upon the deletion of a target object.

Table 3.2 The Major Components of EXPRESS-V

The above mapping languages were mostly based around projects, which required specific pragmatic solutions. The research work carried out in these projects has been valuable, and has shown that the EXPRESS mapping is feasible and indeed desirable.

Following from these efforts, a general mapping language, EXPRESS-X, has been developed. It is based around EXPRESS-V, and also has some features of EXPRESS-M included. It is a structural data mapping language. It consists of language elements that allow unambiguous specification of the relationship between models.

3.3.1 The EXPRESS-X language

EXPRESS-X is a language that maps information between information models. A simple description of it is that it is an upward compatible extension of the EXPRESS language that adds some features of SQL. It has two constructs called VIEW and MAP. The former specifies the alternative views of the data described by an EXPRESS information model. The latter, with the assistance of the former, specifies the transformation of data described by elements of one EXPRESS model into data described by elements of another EXPRESS model.

3.3.1.1 View

VIEW is an alternative organization of the information in an EXPRESS model. The following example includes a schema_2 schema (illustrated in Figure 3.1) in EXPRESS and on associated an example schema_view of the EXPRESS-X language, which consists of a square_from_rectangle view construct. The square_from_rectangle view reorganizes the information in the schema_2 schema.

```
(*This schema is in EXPRESS*)
SCHEMA schema_2;
ENTITY rectangle_2;
    top_left_point : point;
    width : length;
    height : length;
END_ENTITY;
ENTITY point;
    x : length;
    y : length;
END_ENTITY;
TYPE length = REAL;
END_TYPE;
END_SCHEMA;


(*This is a SCHEMA_VIEW in EXPRESS-X*)
SCHEMA_VIEW example;
REFERENCE FROM schema_2;
VIEW square_from_rectangle;
FROM (p: schema_2.rectangle_2);
```

```
WHERE (p.width = p.height)
SELECT
    top_left_point : point := p.top_left_point;
    side_length : length := p.width;
END_VIEW;
END_SCHEMA_VIEW;
```

In the above example, the SCHEMA_VIEW and END_SCHEMA_VIEW define the scope of a VIEW construct. Information in the FROM language element of the VIEW is used to identify the source extents from which the view is established, and also to define some variables for the latter reference. The FROM element in the above example states that the VIEW is established on the rectangle_2 entity in the schema_2 schema. The variable p is defined too; it is bound to the rectangle_2 entity. One or more selection criteria are applied to each of the instances of the viewed model. The selection criteria are defined by the WHERE language element of the view data type. The WHERE language element from the above example defines a selection criterion identifying a subset of the instances. In this case, the subset of instances for which the value of the width attribute of variable p equals the value of the height attribute of variable p. The SELECT language element defines the attributes of VIEW. In the example, the first attribute, top_left_point, receives its value from the top_left_point attribute of variable p; the side_length attribute receives its value from the width attribute of the variable p. The square_from_rectangle view does not provide any supplementary information beyond the schema_2 schema, but filters the squares from the rectangles.

The view constructs do not carry out the mapping by themselves, but assist the map constructs to do so. The view constructs apply some selection, transformation and construction on the mapping source model, and await the invocation from the map constructs. The mapping may be directly from some entities of the source schemas, or from some views of them when the mapping source is not an explicitly defined entity in the source model.

3.3.1.2 Map

The map constructs are the core of the EXPRESS-X language, because they carry out the mapping within the context of the view structures.

The MAP declaration supports the specification of correspondence between semantically equivalent elements of two or more EXPRESS models possessing differing structure. Map is therefore the declaration of a relationship between data of one or more source entity types or view data types and data of one or more target entity types.

A MAP declaration consists of a header and a body. The header identifies target instances to be created and the selection criteria to be applied. The body assigns values to the attributes of these target entities. A MAP construct of the EXPRESS-X language may describe the mapping between the models in Figure 3.1.

```
SCHEMA_MAP rectangle_map;
TARGET tar : schema_2;
SOURCE src : schema_1;
MAP rectangle_to_rectangle AS rectangle_2;
    FROM (p : src.rectangle_1)
SELECT
    rectangle_2.top_left_point := p.top_left_point;
    rectangle_2.width := p.top_left_point.x_p.bottom - right_point.x;
    rectangle_2.height := p.top_left_point.y-p.bottom - right_point.y;
END_MAP;
END_MAP_SCHEMA;
```

In the above example, the SCHEMA_MAP and the END_SCHEMA_MAP declarations define a scope for a collection of related mapping declarations.

In the MAP construct, the header, MAP rectangle_to_rectangle AS rectangle_2 expressed that the mapping target was rectangle_2 entity.

The body of the mapping:

```
FROM (p : src.rectangle_1)
SELECT
    rectangle_2.top_left_point := p.top_left_point;
    rectangle_2.width := p.top_left_point.x - p.bottom_right_point.x;
    rectangle_2.height := p.top_left_point.y - p.bottom_right_point.y;
END_MAP;
```

described how to assign the values of the target instances. In detail, the values of three attributes of the rectangle_2 entity: top_left_point, width and length are computed from the mapping source, the rectangle_1 entity in the schema_1 schema. The top_left_point attribute of the rectangle_2 receives the value of the top_left_point attribute of the p variable. The width attribute of the rectangle_2 entity receives the difference between the values of the x attributes of the top_left_point attribute and the bottom_right_point attribute of the p variable. The height attribute the rectangle_2 entity receives the difference between the values of the y attributes of the top_left_point attribute and the bottom_right_point attribute of the p variable.

The Map constructs identify the target entities in their headers, and then in their bodies, assign values to the attributes of the target entities. The assigned values are computed from the values of the attributes of some entities, which are commonly called mapping source. The Map construct defines the mapping source, the mapping target and the mapping rules, and is the core of the EXPRESS-X mapping language.

3.4 EMM model mapping representation

EMM is a model mapping representation. The original motivation of EMM is to describe the model mapping in a general way, not to tightly bind the mapping specification to a specified mapping language such as EXPRESS-X. One target of this book is to identify the mapping issues when doing model based data translation. Thus it is necessary and helpful to use a general mapping representation to describe the mapping issues and screen them from the differences among the mapping languages.

The mapping description using EMM is at two separate levels, the container level and the data level.

3.4.1 Viewing the mapping from two levels

An information model in EXPRESS describes a domain of interest, including the semantic information and its constitution. The semantic information concentrates on what the model constructs are, regardless of the constructs' internal constitutions. The constructs, hence, look like some opaque containers labelled with their semantics. Their internal constitutions are screened. Therefore the semantics of a model construct is named the container level information in the context of this book. The model constructs in EXPRESS include SCHEMA, ENTITY, ATTRIBUTE and TYPE. The data level information concentrates on the model's constitution and attributes, what ENTITIES are in the SCHEMA, and what each ENTITY consists of.

For example, consider the rectangle_1 entity in the schema_1 schema in Figure 3.1 again. Table 3.3 shows that the information the rectangle_1 entity holds may be classified into a container part and a data part. The rectangle_1 entity, as a whole, defines the rectangle concept in the geometry world at the container level. At the data level, it has two attributes: top_left_point and bottom_right_point. When considering an entity at the container level, it is unnecessary to consider what attributes and constraints it has. The top_left_point and the bottom_right_point attributes define the top-left point and the bottom-right point of a rectangle at the container level. At the data level, these two attributes must receive the values of the point data type.

Entity	Attribute	Container Information	Data Information
`rectangle_1`		Rectangle in the graphic world	It consists of two attributes: `top_left_point` and `bottom_right_point`
	`top_left_point : point;`	The top left point of a rectangle	The data type of the values that this attribute can receive must be `point`.
	`bottom_right_point : point`	The bottom right point of a rectangle	The data type of the values that this attribute can receive must be `point`.

Table 3.3 The Semantic and Data Information of the `rectangle_1`

Information models focus on the semantics; the information model mapping therefore is decided by the semantics of the source model and the target model. In other words, the container level information directs the mapping. For example, consider the `rectangle_1` entity in the `schema_1` schema and the `rectangle_2` entity in the `schema_2` schema in Figure 3.1 again. The mapping from the `rectangle_1` entity to the `rectangle_2` entity is built because of their information at the container level; both look like a container labelled "rectangle in the 2D graphic world". If the attributes of the `rectangle_1` entity changed, perhaps a `centre_point` attribute takes the place of the `bottom_right_point` attribute, the `rectangle_1` entity will still be mapped to the `rectangle_2` entity, because the `rectangle_1` entity is still a container labelled "rectangle in the 2D graphics world", although the contents of the container has been changed.

On the other hand, the existing mapping will be broken, if the container level information of the source or target changed, although the data information remains unchanged. For example, still consider the `rectangle_1` entity in the `schema_1` schema and the `rectangle_2` entity in the `schema_2` schema in Figure 3.1. If the `rectangle_1` entity changes to a `circle` entity, while the `top_left_point` and `bottom_right_point` attributes remains unchanged (because the new `circle` entity has a `top_left_point` attribute and a `bottom_right_point` attribute, which define a circle in the 2D graphic world by its tangential square.), it will become unreasonable to map the `circle` entity that has replaced the `rectangle_1` entity to the `rectangle_2` entity, because the `circle` entity, at the contain level, is a container labelled "circle in the 2D graphic world". The container level information of the `rectangle_1` entity and the `circle` entity are different, though they have the same information at the data level.

Then the mapping may also be specified at two levels. What is the mapping source and target is decided by the semantics of the models. The container level of the EMM will carry out this task. The data level, stepping into the insides of the mapped entities, specifies the mapping detail according to the entities' structure or constitution.

The data level mapping concentrates on how to map data instances. Since the mapping source and target are already decided at the container level, the data level defines some data processing rules to implement in detail the requirements that are set at the container level.

3.4.2 The structure of EMM

EMM precisely follows the idea of the two-level mapping, and views mapping at both the container level and the data level.

An EMM mapping specification always consists of some mapping units. Each unit describes the mapping at two levels. All mapping units, combined or nested together, form the mapping between two models as a whole. Figure 3.4 illustrates some mapping units.

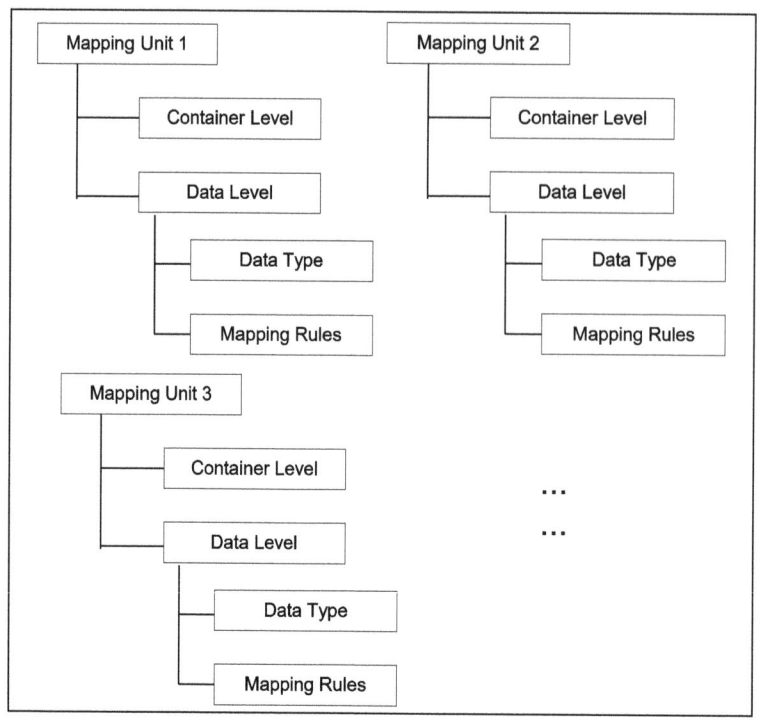

Figure 3.4 Illustration of Structure of EMM

The mapping between the two models of rectangle in Figure 3.1 can be described in EMM. Below is the mapping description in EMM.

```
Mapping Unit ID: rectangle_to_rectangle;
Container level:
    Source: schema_1.rectangle_1;
    Target: schema_2.rectangle_2;
Data level:
    Source data type: rectangle_1 entity data type in schema_1;
    Target data type: rectangle_2 entity data type in schema_2;
    Mapping rules:
    rectangle_2 = new rectangle_2 (
point_to_point(schema_1.rectangle_1.top_left_point),
(schema_1.rectangle_1.top_left_point.x-
schema_1.rectangle_1.bottom_right_point.x),
(schema_1.rectangle_1.top_left_point.y-
schema_1.rectangle_1.bottom_right_point.y));


Mapping Unit ID: point_to_point;
Container level:
    Source: schema_1.rectangle_1.top_left_point;
Target: schema_2.rectangle_2.top_left_point;
Data level:
    Source data type: point entity data type in schema_1;
    Target data type: point entity data type in schema_2;
    Mapping rules:
```

```
    schema_2.rectangle_2.top_left_point = new point(
schema_1.rectangle_1.top_left_point.x,
schema_1.rectangle_1.top_left_point.y);
```

There are two mapping units in the above mapping description. The first one, whose identification is `rectangle_to_rectangle`, maps the `rectangle_1` entity in `schema_1` to `rectangle_2` in `schema_2`. The second one, whose identification is `point_to_point`, maps the `point` entity in `schema_1` to the `point` entity in `schema_2`.

3.4.3 Mapping unit

Each mapping unit consists of a container level specification and a data level specification. These two levels, cooperating with each other, describe the source, the target and the mapping rules.

3.4.3.1 Container level mapping

In the above example, at the container level, a mapping unit creates a link between the entities of the source model and target model that are semantically related. The created link represents the semantics of the current mapping unit. The entities in the mapping source and target are identified by the following rules:

1. The schema the entity is in.

2. The position in the hierarchy of model the entity is in.

3. The name of the entity.

What is not under consideration is the constitution of the entity, such as what attributes it has. In `rectangle_to_rectangle` mapping unit, no matter what attributes the `rectangle_1` and `rectangle_2` entities have, the mapping must exist between them. It is caused by their semantics; it does not concern their data types.

Compared with the following data level mapping, the container level is the higher in the structure of a mapping unit. The link created at this level is inexact; it only notes what are included in this mapping unit. In other words, this level draws out the domain of this mapping unit. In the mentioned three aspects of a mapping, the mapping source, the mapping target, and the mapping rule, the container level specifies the first two.

3.4.3.2 Data level mapping

The upper level, the container level, defines the source and target of a mapping unit. At the data level, the mapping rules between source and target should be defined more precisely.

1. Data type specification

In order to precisely describe the mapping rules, it is necessary first to clarify the data types. The upper level specifies what the source and the target are; this level specifies their data types. For example, the data level of the `rectangle_to_rectangle` mapping unit defines that the data type of the source is the `rectangle_1` entity data type in `schema_1`, and the data type of target is the `rectangle_2` entity data type in `schema_2`. These two specifications, working together, provide a very clear definition of the source and target of the current mapping unit.

2. Mapping rule specification

Since the data types are already clarified, the mapping rules specification defines the transforming methods from the data types of the source to the ones of the target. Such methods include how to generate some new objects that conform to the data types of the mapping target based on the objects of the mapping source and how to update the existing objects in the mapping target according the mapping source. For example, in mapping unit `rectangle_to_rectangle` (in Section 3.4.2), the mapping rule describes, in detail, how to generate a `rectangle_2` object based on the available `rectangle_1` object.

The common manipulation methods such as object generation, value assignment, iteration and selection are available in the mapping rules specification. The mapping rule specifications in EMM are effectively pseudo-code for the purpose of implementation convenience, and the available manipulation methods are the same as the ones of the Java language.

The mapping rules in the mapping units `rectangle_to_rectangle` and `point_to_point` are described using some Java pseudo code, because the Java language is selected for implementing them and for processing model mappings in the context of this book. The mapping rules could also have been described in some other pseudo-codes such as C pseudo-code, C++ pseudo-code or Pascal pseudo-code.

At the data level, the instance data of the models are identified by their data types. The semantics are not in consideration. No matter what role they play in the model, they will be processed according to the mapping rules, if they match the data type identification.

3.4.4 Relationship between mapping units

The mapping rule specifications in a mapping unit can invoke other mapping units. When specify the mapping between attributes, it will lead to use the mapping between the entities that the attributes are of type of. In the `rectangle_to_rectangle` mapping unit, the mapping rule specification invokes the `point_to_point` mapping unit in order to specify the mapping between their attributes such as `top_left_point`. If the mapping unit is complex, its mapping rules are complicated and it is likely to invoke other mapping units. In other words, a mapping unit can be decomposed to some other ones.

3.4.5 Comparison between the EMM and EXPRESS-X

EMM is an information model mapping specification method. EXPRESS-X is a data mapping language, and the data are denoted as an ordered set of entity instance names (see ISO standard 10303-11 clause 7.3.4 [ISO94b]) separated by commas "," and enclosed in angle brackets "<>" [ISO99]. In brief, EMM defines the mapping conceptually, without considering the implementation, whereas EXPRESS-X depicts the mapping of the model instances that are in a specified format. EXPRESS-X is an optional approach to implement the mapping specification in EMM.

In this book, EMM only specifies the mapping on the ENTITY/ATTRIBUTE level. EMM can do at other levels such as the model/SCHEMA level and the SCHEMA/ENTITY level, because at the container level in EMM, a container can be a model, a SCHEMA or an ENTITY. The MAP and VIEW constructs of EXPRESS-X can only work on ENTITIES.

3.5 The model mapping methods in the UML family and the XML family

There are some mapping methods and languages in the UML family and the XML family.

Now the OMG group has moved its focus to Model Driven Architecture (MDA) [MDA]. Since models play a very important role in MDA to build software systems, model mapping will occur very frequently and is worthy studying. In that context, the models in MDA are specified in the UML language. The issue therefore is how to specify the model mapping using UML language too, no specified details have yet been found.

The Extensible Stylesheet Language Transformation (XSLT) [W3Ce] can specify the transformation between XML files. The XSLT extensions allow the approach to be used beyond the XML family, and can describe the transformation between a range of different types of file and can therefore be considered as a way of mapping. The XSLT's idea is to generate some tree like structures based on the input files during run time, scan the structures and identify the matched nodes, and transform the nodes to generate some new tree like structures. The cardinalities of the input and output tree like structures are variable. XSLT can handle the one-to-one case very well, but plays quite poor in the multiple-to-multiple case. XSLT's applicability to EXPRESS model mapping requires further consideration.

3.6 Conclusions

This chapter introduced the concept of mapping between information models, its targets, its contents and its requirements.

Some EXPRESS-related information model mapping languages, such as EXPRESS-V, EXPRESS-M and

EXPRESS-X are introduced.

A new EXPRESS model mapping specification method, called EMM, is introduced. It will be used in the examples in Chapter 5 and Chapter 6.

At present EMM is only a draft. Some other aspects such as conditional mapping and partial mapping have not been addressed. It is only a trial encoding of the mapping in the field of data translation. In the future, more work will be done on EMM. Finally, it will be able to address the issues of the complicated mapping introduced in Chapter 1.

Chapter 4 SVG and its information model

The research on data translation is based on a concrete case: Translation and representation of 2D graphical data. In Chapters 2 and 3, the key methods, information modelling and model mapping were introduced. Before the focus moves to the worked examples, Scalable Vector Graphics (SVG) and its information model should be introduced. SVG is used directly in two worked examples: a Gerber-To-SVG translator and an AGS-To-SVG translator. In both examples, SVG is treated as the general 2D graphical data format to which the source data are translated. SVG is selected as the data repository and representation format because it is a member of the XML family of standards, which offers a very suitable basis for web based messaging, presentation and representation and as such is a useful target.

4.1 Introduction to SVG

SVG is a language for describing 2 dimensional graphics in XML. Basic shapes, paths and texts are available in SVG, and these graphical objects can be grouped, styled, transformed and composed into the rendered objects [W3Cb].

To be scalable means to increase or decrease uniformly. In terms of graphics, scalable means not being limited to a single, fixed, pixel size. SVG graphics are scalable to different display resolutions, so that for example printed output uses the full resolution of the printer and the graphics can be displayed at the same size on screens of different resolutions [W3Cb].

Vector graphics contains geometric objects such as lines and curves. This gives great flexibility compared with the raster-only formats (such as Portable Network Graphics (PNG) [PNG] and Joint Picture Expert Group (JPEG) [IJG]), which have to store information for every pixel of the graphical image. Typically, vector formats can also integrate raster images and can combine them with vector information such as clipping paths to produce a complete illustration; SVG is a good case in point.

SVG drawing can be interactive and dynamic. Animation can be defined and triggered either declaratively by embedding SVG animation elements in an SVG fragment or via scripting.

SVG is a member of the XML family, or in other words, SVG itself is an XML application. An SVG file is already an XML file. Tools that are developed for XML may be applied to SVG also. This greatly reduces the burden on developers wishing to process SVG data.

4.2 The structure of an SVG model

The SVG language covers a great deal about 2D graphics, such as graphic element definition, manipulation and styling. Moreover, SVG is dynamic and interactive; it covers animation and the interactivity with the end-users.

Although it is possible to press and pack the whole SVG model into a single schema, it is better to split the model and assign it into a few schemas. If the SVG model is in a single schema, the USE/REFERENCE interfaces between schemas will become unnecessary and can be omitted. Hence, the structure of the SVG model will become simpler. However, the single schema SVG model is not sufficient to depict the infrastructure of the SVG language, especially the modules of the SVG language. Therefore, the SVG language, from the view of its semantics, is too complicated to be modelled in a single schema. Moreover, the SVG language is open; some other technologies such as Cascading Style Sheet (CSS) can be plugged into the SVG language. It also requires the SVG model to be separated into a few schemas for pluggability. The SVG information model produced in support of this work is divided into a number of EXPRESS schemas. These are based on the semantics of SVG and on 2D graphics conventions. The SVG information model is divided into six schemas:

```
Svg_Geometry_Model,
Svg_Structure_Model,
```

```
Svg_Presentation_Model,
Svg_Interactivity_Model,
Svg_Animation_Model,
Svg_External_Model.
```

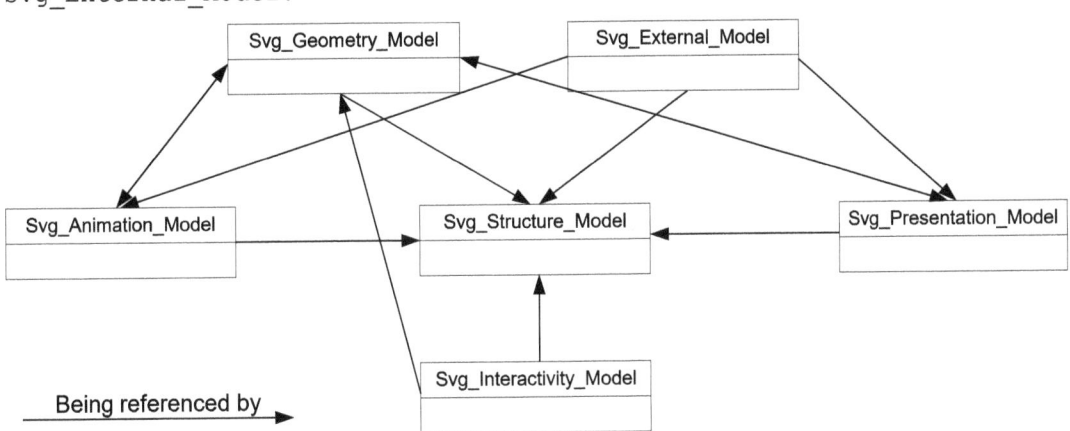

Figure 4.1 References among the SVG Model Schemas

The `Svg_Geometry_Model` schema is the basis of the SVG model, and it defines some basic geometry concepts such as coordinate, angle, point, line, circle and path. It also covers the geometrical transformations, such as translate, rotate and skew, which can be applied on the geometrical entities. In Figure 4.1, the `Svg_Structure_Model` schema references the basic geometrical entities in the `Svg_Geometry_Model` schema and uses them to construct its contents. The `Svg_Animation_Model` schema and the `Svg_Presentation_Model` schema reference the basic geometrical entities and use them as some sort of assistance too. For example, the `Svg_Presentation_Model` schema references the `rectangle` entity in the `Svg_Geometry_Model` to define its `pattern` entity, `marker` entity and `filter` entity. The `animation` entity in the `Svg_Animation_Model` schema references the `path` entity in the `Svg_Geometry_Model` schema to define its animation path.

The `Svg_Structure_Model` schema is the core of the SVG model. An SVG file may consist of many graphic units, and they may be grouped and characterized. It may also reuse some resources that are not in it. The `Svg_Structure_Model` schema in Figure 4.1 defines the structure of the SVG files. It references the basic geometrical entities from the `Svg_Geometry_Model`, organizes and integrates them, and assigns them some presentation attributes, which are referenced from the `Svg_Presentation_Model` schema.

The `Svg_Presentation_Model` defines the presentation attributes for SVG files. There are various presentation attributes such as line width, background colour and patterns or gradients for stroking and filling. The schema references some information from the `Svg_Geometry_Model` and the `Svg_External_Model` to define the presentation attributes. The presentation attributes will then be referenced by the geometrical entities of the `Svg_Geometry_Model` or the groups of the graphic units in the `Svg_Structure_Model` schema. For example, the `pattern` entity, which is in the `Svg_Presentation_Model` schema, can use some `rectangle` entities to define its attributes, and then apply itself to another `rectangle` entity.

The `Svg_Animation_Model` defines the SVG's animation ability. It uses some basic geometrical entities to define the animation path. The geometrical entities and the groups of geometrical entities may reference some animation entities to achieve dynamic effects on screen. This schema has not been finished when composing the book.

The `Svg_Interactivity_Model` defines the interactivity between SVG files and end-users. From Figure 4.1, only the entities in the `Svg_Geometry_Model` and the `Svg_Structure_Model` schemas can achieve the interactivity.

The `Svg_External_Model` is an auxiliary schema. It defines some information about end-users' computers and some other useful standards such as URI. In fact it does not really cover the model of URI, but simplifies it to a string only for the purpose of EXPRESS syntax checking. The end-users' information includes the resolution and the colour representation abilities of the end-users' machines.

Each of the above six schemas depicts an aspect of the information about SVG from a specific perspective. All of them, taken together, cover all the information capability of SVG without overlap.

4.3 Some other modelling issues

Some rules are applied in modelling the SVG language. They are not mandatory in the EXPRESS language, but are adopted here as conventions.

4.3.1 ABSTRACT SUPERTYPES

The `SUPERTYPE/SUBTYPE` structure is heavily used to express the generalization/specialization relationship in the SVG model. In order to clarify the hierarchical structure of the model and the relationships between the entities, a convention, that all `SUPERTYPE` entities must be `ABSTRACT`, is applied in the SVG model. The `angle` entity introduced in Section 4.4.1.1 is an example.

4.3.2 INVERSE attributes and existence dependencies

In an EXPRESS model, if another entity has established a relationship with the current entity by way of an explicit attribute, an inverse attribute may be used to describe that relationship in the context of the current entity. Although the inverse attributes may be used to express many kinds of relationships such as reference, a convention that all inverse attributes must be used to describe the existence dependency relationships is applied in modelling the SVG language. Moreover, all non-stand-alone entities must have inverse attributes to define their existence dependencies. If an entity has multiple inverse attributes, it must have a `WHERE` rule to constrain these attributes, because the existences of the inverse attributes of an entity are mutually exclusive; an instance of a specified entity can have only one `INVERSE` attribute. The `coordinate` entity in Section 4.4.1.3 is a case in point.

4.4 Svg_Geometry_Model

In the `Svg_Geometry_Model` schema, the information about the basic geometry data types, basic shapes, path, text and the transformation of graphic elements is introduced. The named data types defined in this schema will be referenced or used by the other schemas. The full schema is presented in Appendix 1.

4.4.1 Basic geometry data types

SVG's basic geometry data types include angle, length, coordinate and point.

4.4.1.1 Angle

In the SVG language, an angle is measured using degrees, grads, or radians. The default measurement unit is degrees.

In the SVG model, an abstract supertype entity `angle` is defined, which has three subtypes: `angleInRadian`, `angleInDegree` and `angleInGrad` (See Figure 4.2). All `INVERSE` attributes of the `angle` entity are omitted in the EXPRESS-G diagram in Figure 4.2, for the compactness. The `angle` supertype entity has only one attribute `angleValueInRadian`, which is redeclared in its subtype entities: `angleInDegree` and `angleInGrad`. The subtype `angleInDegree` has a private attribute `angleValueInDegree` and the subtype `angleValueInGrad` has a private attribute `angleValueInGrad`. These two subtypes redeclare the inherited attribute `angleValueInRadian`, and the redeclaration is based on the transformation between the inherited attribute and the private ones. Another subtype `angleInRadian` has no private attributes and is identical to its supertype. Hence each subtype represents a concept of angle measured using a specific unit. No matter what unit a subtype of `angle` carries, it can be transformed to an angle value in radians. This provides a way of transforming between different angle units.

The `angleInRadian` entity and its supertype have the same attributes. It is also possible to delete the `angleInRadian` entity and make its supertype, `angle`, non `ABSTRACT`. However, the current version can describe the generalization/specialization relationships more precisely. The `angle` entity is a general concept, and is abstract. It has three more specific forms, the `angleInRadian`, the `angleInDegree` and the `angleInGrad` entities. It is an example of the convention introduced in Section 4.3.1.

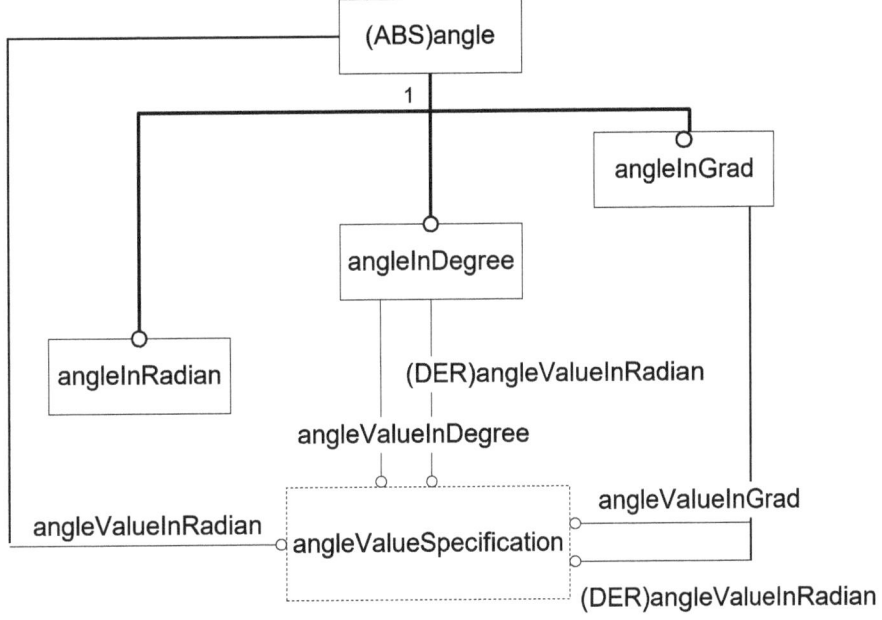

Figure 4.2 The `Angle` Entity

4.4.1.2 Length

A length is a distance measurement. The length measurement in SVG can be in terms of pixels, ems, exs, points, picas, centimetres, millimetres or percentage of a view port (where a view port simply equates to a window). The EXPRESS entity for the above concept of length in the SVG model is called `svgLength`, because length is a reserved word in the EXPRESS language.

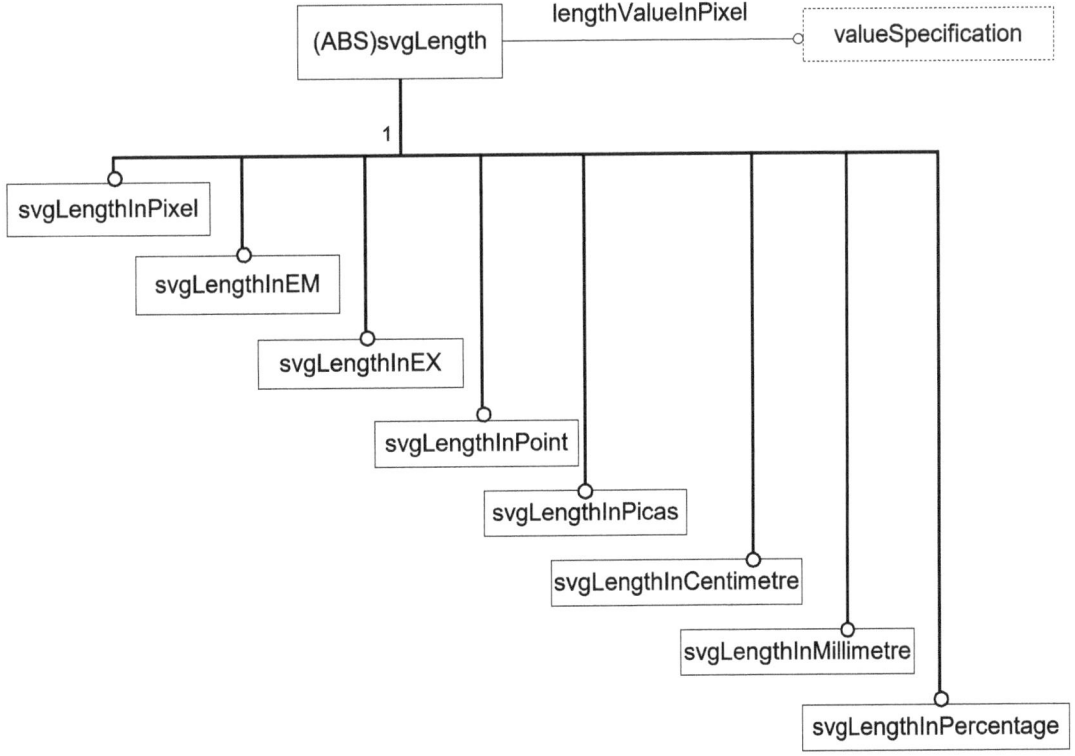

Figure 4.3 The `Svglength` Entity

This entity is an abstract supertype (See Figure 4.3), and each of its concrete subtypes records a length value using a specified unit, such as pixel, point, and centimetre. The entity `svgLength` has an attribute `lengthValueInPixel`, which is common to all its subtypes. Each subtype has its own attribute, which records the length value using the measurement that the subtype itself carries. Moreover, the common attribute `lengthValueInPixel` will be redeclared on the computation of the private attributes. The length value measured in pixels is identified as a common attribute of all the subtypes, because no matter what units are used, an `svgLength` entity is finally rendered to the screen in pixel units.

Figure 4.2 does not represent the INVERSE attributes describe the existence dependency.

4.4.1.3 Coordinate

Because coordinates in SVG can be absolute or relative, a supertype-subtype structure is built to express this concept and relationship. The `coordinate` entity is an abstract supertype (See Figure 4.4), which has two concrete subtypes: `absoluteCoordinate` and `relativeCoordinate`. The entity `absoluteCoordinate` does not have any attributes except the ones inherited from its supertype. However, the `relativeCoordinate` entity additionally has its own attribute `lastCoordinate`, which is the origin for the relative coordinate computation.

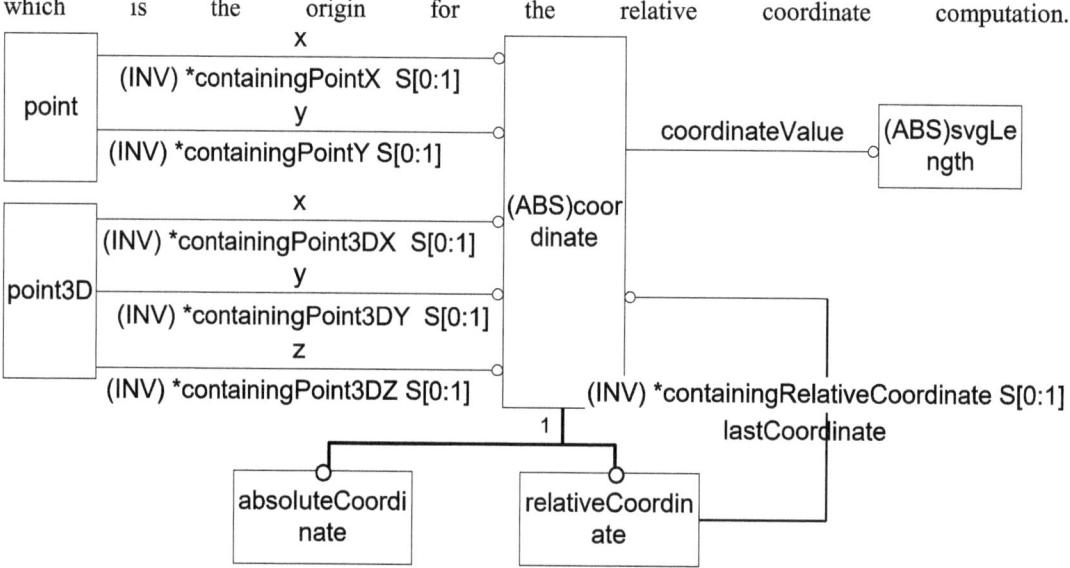

Figure 4.4 The `Point` and `Coordinate` Entities

The existence of an instance of the `coordinate` entity is dependent on the x or y attributes of the `point` entity, or the x or y or z attributes of the `point3D` entity. In order to describe the existence dependence of the `coordinate` entity, it has five INVERSE attributes and a WHERE rules on them, shown in the following paragraph. The `validExistence` defines a constraint that to each instance of the `coordinate` entity, it must have one and only one INVERSE attribute. This is an example of the convention introduced in Section 4.3.2.

```
ENTITY coordinate
    ...
INVERSE
    containingPointX: SET [0:1] of point FOR x;
    containingPointY: SET [0:1] of point FOR y;
    containingPoint3DX: SET [0:1] of point3D FOR x;
    containingPoint3DY: SET [0:1] of point3D FOR y;
    containingPoint3DZ: SET [0:1] of point3D FOR z;
    containingRelativeCoordinate : SET [0:1] OF relativeCoordinate FOR lastCoordinate;
```

```
WHERE
    validExistence : SIZEOF (containingPointX) +
                SIZEOF (containingPointY)  +
                SIZEOF (containingPoint3DX) +
                SIZEOF (containingPoint3DY) +
                SIZEOF (containingPoint3DZ) +
SIZEOF (containingRelativeCoordinate)  =1;
END_ENTITY;
```

4.4.1.4 Point

In most graphical languages, a point plays the role of a basic shape, not a basic data type. However, the SVG language does not regard it as a basic shape, which means that a single point cannot be drawn in the SVG world. In the SVG language a point can only exist as a subcomponent of some basic shape, such as the start/end of a line, or the centre of a circle.

The model of point (See Figure 4.4) is relatively simple, an entity with two attributes, which represent the pair of coordinates. The coordinates may be absolute or relative. The point3D entity, which has x, y and z attributes, does not intend to include the point in three dimension world. It only serves for the three-dimension-lighting approximation, which is defined in Svg_Presenation_Model schema.

4.4.2 Basic shape

The SVG language offers the following set of basic shape elements:

Rectangle (including square corner ones and rounded corner ones)

Circle

Ellipse

Line

Polyline

Polygon

Mathematically, these shape elements are equivalent to a path element that would construct the same shape. In the SVG model, an abstract supertype entity basicShape (See Figure 4.5) is created. Transformation, some presentation attributes, animation and interactivity can be assigned to the basicShape entity. It has six subtypes which depict the above six types of special basic shape. The subtype entities not only have the attributes inherited from their supertypes, but also some private ones that define their geometric characteristics. For example, the circle entity has an attribute to define its centre, and another one for its radius. The definition to the container entity can be found in the Svg_Structure_model schema (See Section 4.5).

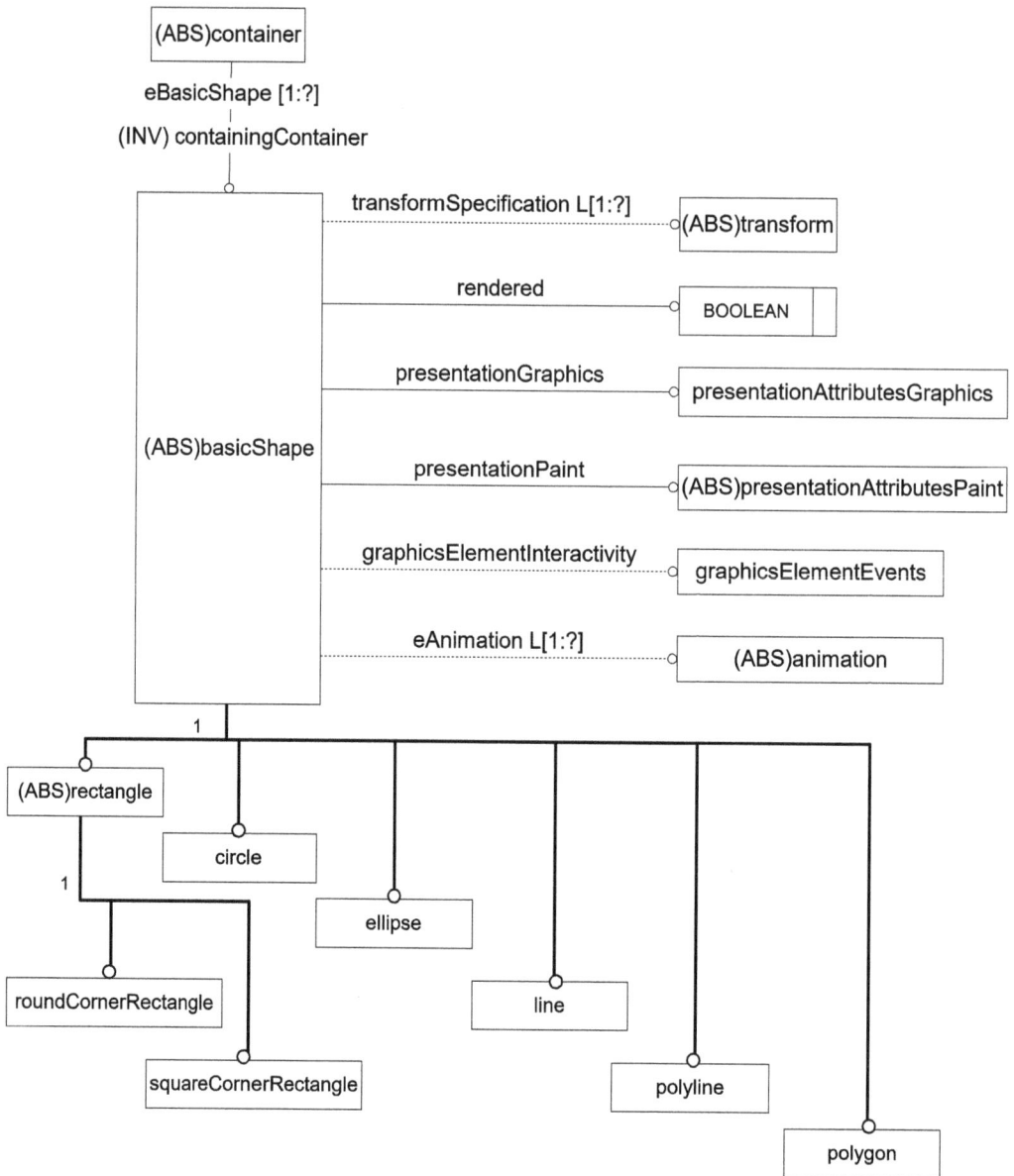

Figure 4.5 The `BasicShape` Entity

4.4.3 Path

The basic geometry element of SVG is a path; even the basic shapes consist of some paths. A path is a list of line segments, Bezier curves (including cubic Bezier and quadratic Bezier curves) and arcs. A path can be closed or open.

A path can be nested. A subpath can be separated from the path that nests it. So it is possible to define something like a donut hole.

A path is described using the concept of a current point. In an analogy with drawing on paper, the current point can be thought of as the pen. The position of the pen can be changed, and the outline of a shape (open or closed) can be traced by dragging the pen either in straight lines or in curves.

In the SVG language, paths represent the geometry of the outline of an object, defined in terms of some commands (See Table 4.1). A description of a path using the above commands is dynamic, which cannot be modelled directly, because an information model always views the world statically rather than in terms of behaviour.

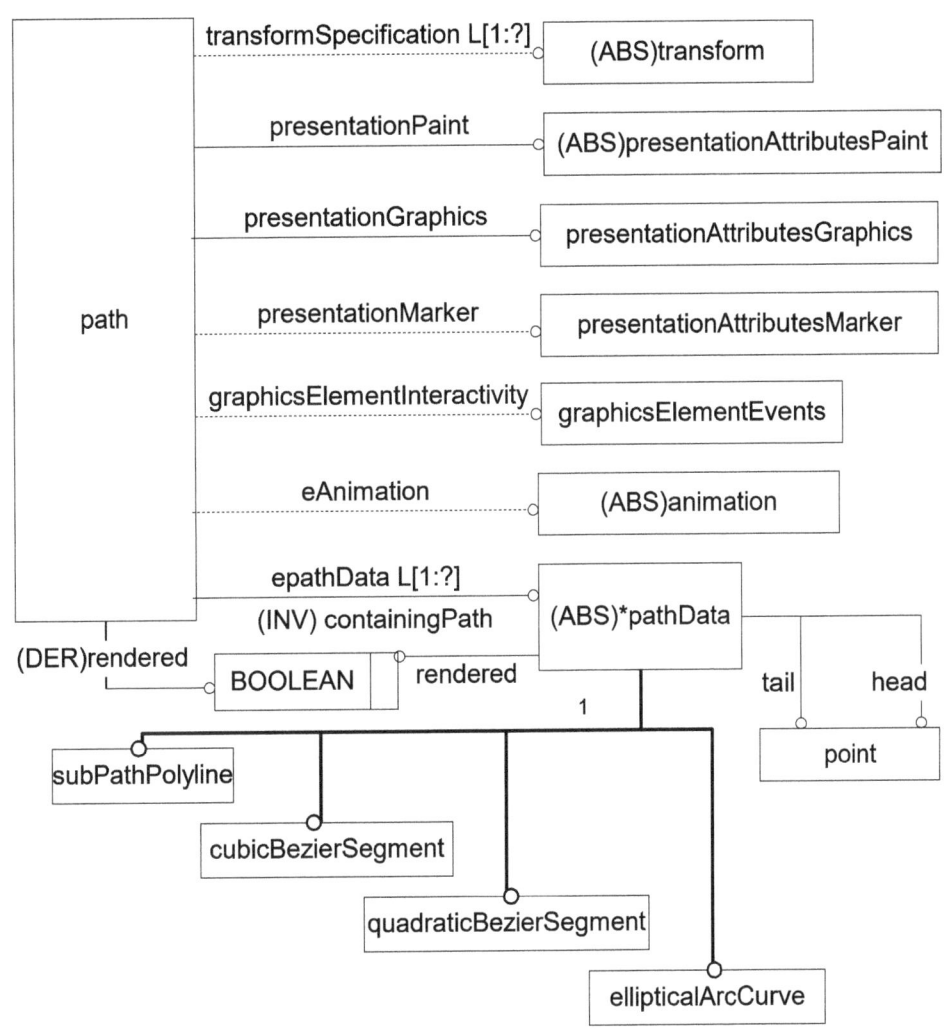

In the SVG model, a `pathData` entity in Figure 4.6 is built to express the above commands. It gives the dynamic path commands static definitions. The `pathData` entity is an abstract supertype of all sorts of mathematically specialized path data, such as: `subPathPolyline`, `cubicBezierSegment`, `quadraticBezierSegment` and `ellipticalArcCurve`. It has two attributes `head` and `tail`, which can be used to specify the starting and ending point of the `pathData`. The `path` entity in Figure 4.6 consists of several `pathData`, as well as some presentation attributes, transformation, animation and interactivity.

Command	Description
moveto	Set a new current point.
lineto	Draw a straight line from the current point to the point specified as the parameter of the command.
curveto	Draw a curve from the current point to the point specified as the parameter of the command, using Bezier method.
arc	Draw an elliptical arc from the current point to the point specified as the parameter of the command.
closepath	Close the current path by drawing a line to the last move to command.

Table 4.1 Path Command

4.4.4 Text

A piece of text that is to be rendered as part of an SVG document fragment is specified using a text element, this is captured in the text entity in the SVG model.

In the SVG model, the text entity is built like the other graphic entities, characterised by its location, font and some other presentation attributes.

4.4.5 Transformation of graphic elements

Transformations map coordinates and lengths from a previous coordinate system into a new one. All graphic elements in SVG can be transformed, and the transformation is split into: translate, scale, rotate, skewX, skewY and generalTransformation (See Figure 4.7).

Mathematically, all transformations can be represented as 3*3 transformation matrices of the following form [W3Cb]:

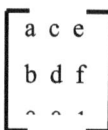

Hence, the transform entity has only the matrix attribute. The data type of the matrix attribute is a multi-dimensioned array.

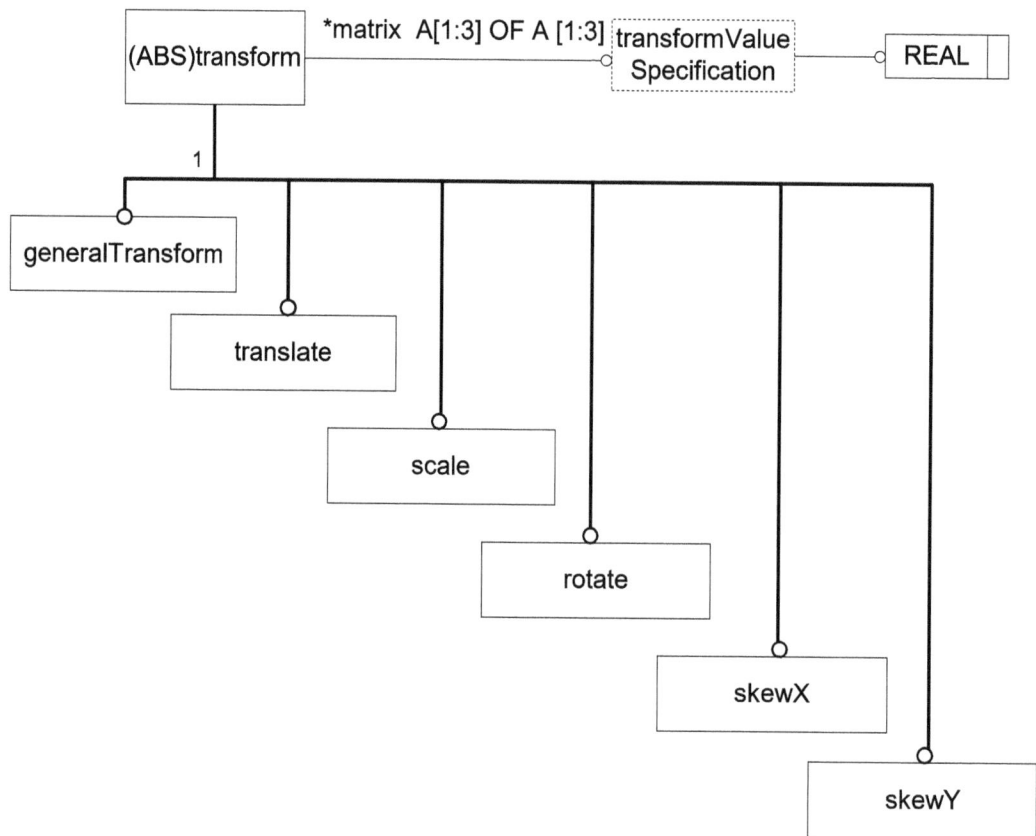

Figure 4.7 The Transform Entity

4.5 Svg_Structure_Model

This schema is the core part of the SVG model, which covers the structure of an SVG document fragment and the reuse mechanism. The full schema is presented in Appendix 2.

4.5.1 Structure of SVG document fragments

An SVG document fragment consists of any number of SVG elements contained within an SVG element. It can range from an empty fragment, to a very simple SVG document fragment containing a single SVG graphics element, to a very complex, deeply nested collection of container elements and graphics elements.

In the SVG language many sorts of elements can work as a container. Thus, an element can have graphics elements and other container element as child elements. To model this, a `container` entity is built. The `container` entity, shown in Figure 4.8, is an abstract supertype entity. Many types of entity, which can carry other containers or graphic entities, are its subtypes, such as the `svgElement` entity and the `group` entity. The `container` entity does not define any INVERSE attributes, but leave them to its subtype entities.

The `svgElement` is ABSTRACT, and it has two subtype entities: the `outMostSvgElement` entity and the `subSvglement` entity. The structure of an SVG document fragment in the SVG model is tree like. The root of the tree is the `outMostSvgElement` entity, which consists of many other containers such as `group`, `symbol`, `subSvgElement`, and some graphics entities such as `basicShape` and `path`. The sub-containers of the root carry other containers and graphics entities as their subcomponents.

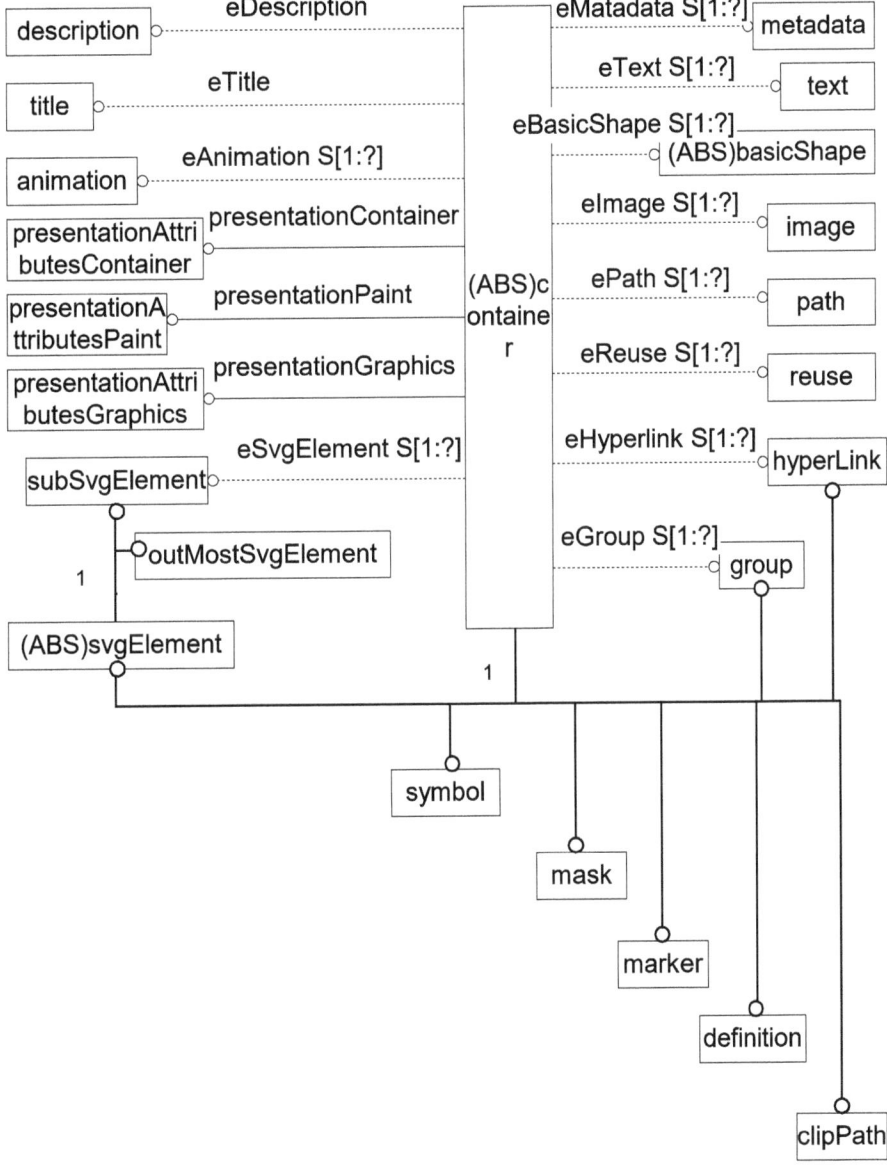

Figure 4.8 The `Container` Entity

4.5.2 Reuse mechanism of SVG

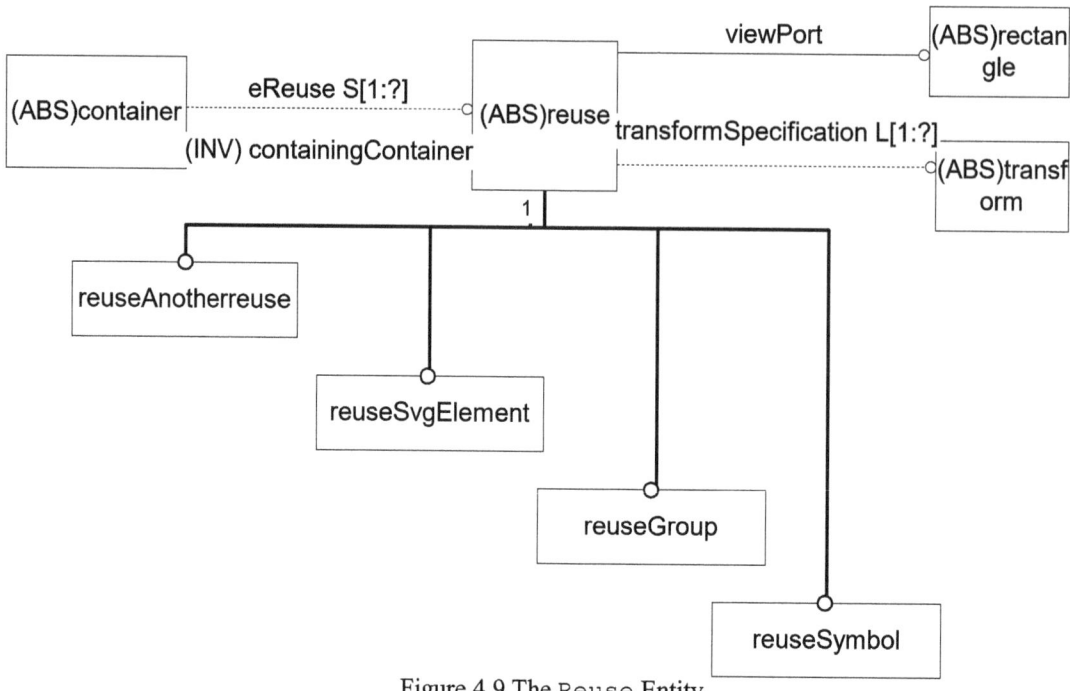

Figure 4.9 The Reuse Entity

The SVG language offers a reuse mechanism (See Figure 4.9). For example, a group or an svg element can be reused in the same SVG fragment. The names of the referenced entities play the role of referencing identifications.

4.6 Svg_Presentation_Model

The SVG language uses styling properties to describe many of its document parameters. Styling properties define how the graphics elements in the SVG content are to be rendered. SVG uses styling properties for the following:

1. Parameters that are clearly visual in nature and thus lend themselves to styling. Examples include all attributes that define how an object is "painted", such as fill and stroke colors, line widths and dash styles.
2. Parameters having to do with text styling such as font-family and font-size.
3. Parameters which impact the way that graphical elements are rendered, such as specifying clipping paths, masks, arrowheads, markers and filter effects.

Styling properties can be assigned to SVG element in the following two ways:

1. Presentation attributes.
2. Cascading Style Sheet (CSS) [W3Cc].

Because the use of CSS is independent of SVG and XML, it is not included in the SVG model.

An Svg_Presentation_Attributes schema is created to carry the information about SVG presentation attributes. It contains some specified presentation attribute definitions.

4.6.1 Container attributes

Container attributes (See Figure 4.10) exist for all sorts of container entities. They provide a way of handling the existing background in the created container entities.

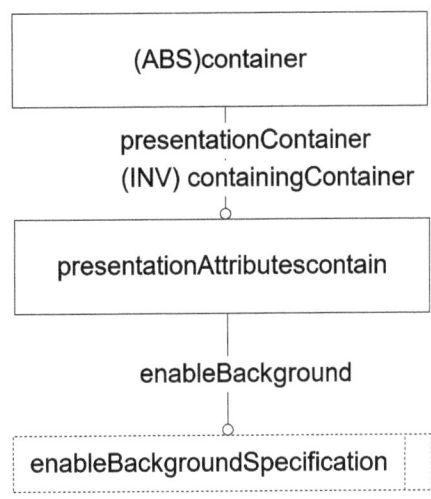

Figure 4.10 Presentation Attributes Container

4.6.2 Paint attributes

All SVG graphics entities can be painted. Painting, in the context of SVG, means filling, stroking or both (See Figure 4.11).

4.6.3 Graphic attributes

The `presentationAttributesGraphics` entity (See Figure 4.12) models all presentation attributes shared by all graphics elements and container elements. Examples here include colour, opacity, and filter.

4.6.4 Marker attributes

The marker attribute (See Figure 4.13) is a special presentation attribute for `line`, `polyline`, `polygon` and `path` entities. It assigns marker symbols, such as arrowheads, to the above-mentioned graphics elements.

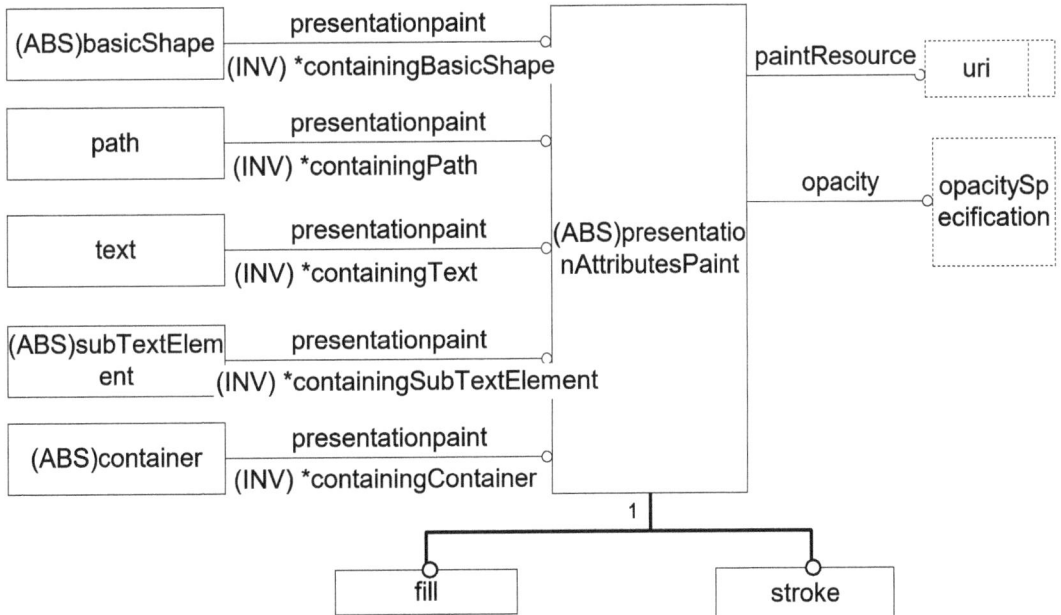

Figure 4.11 Presentation Attributes Paint

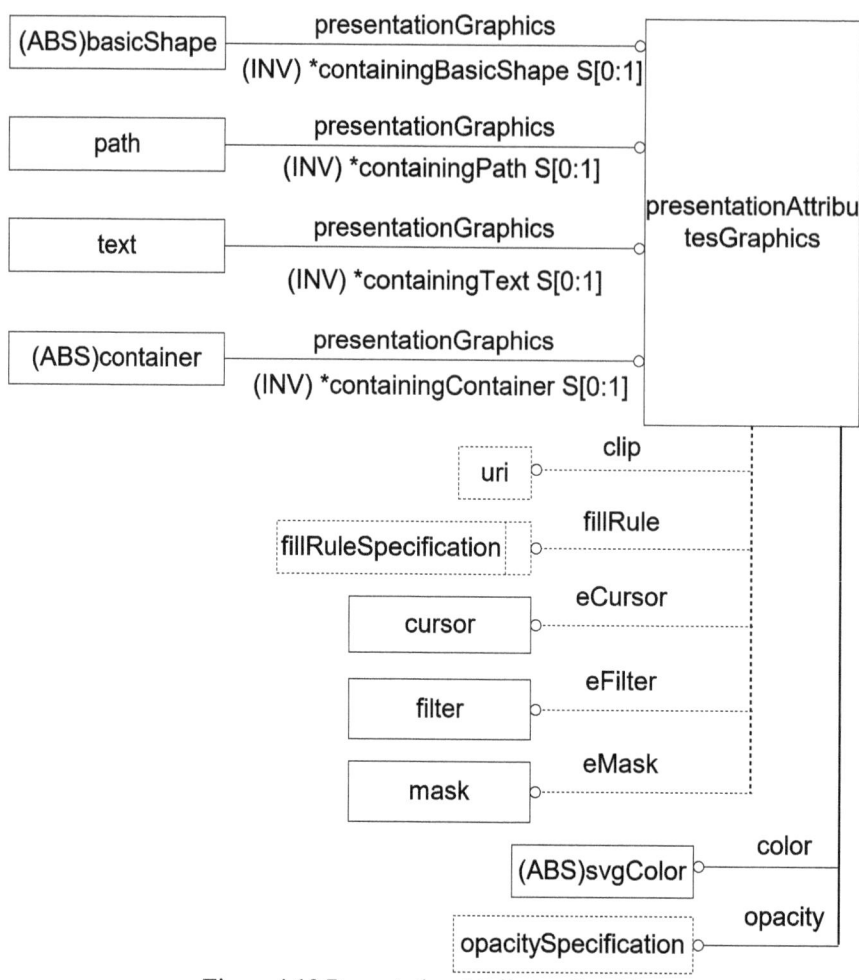

Figure 4.12 Presentation Attributes Graphics

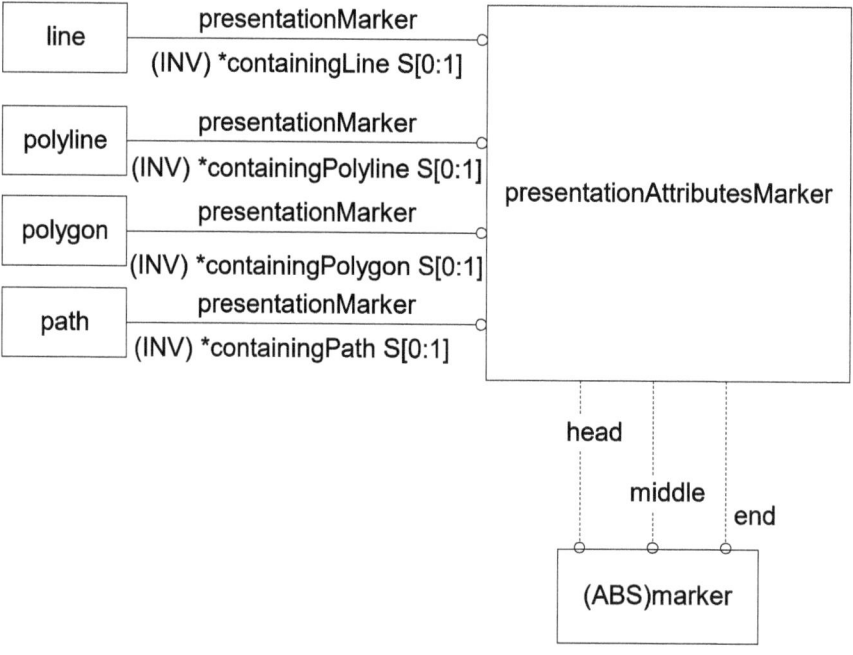

Figure 4.13 Presentation Attributes Marker

4.6.5 Font selection attributes

Font Selection (See Figure 4.14) is a special presentation attribute for text. It assigns a font to the referring entity according to the font selecting attributes such as font family, font size, and font style.

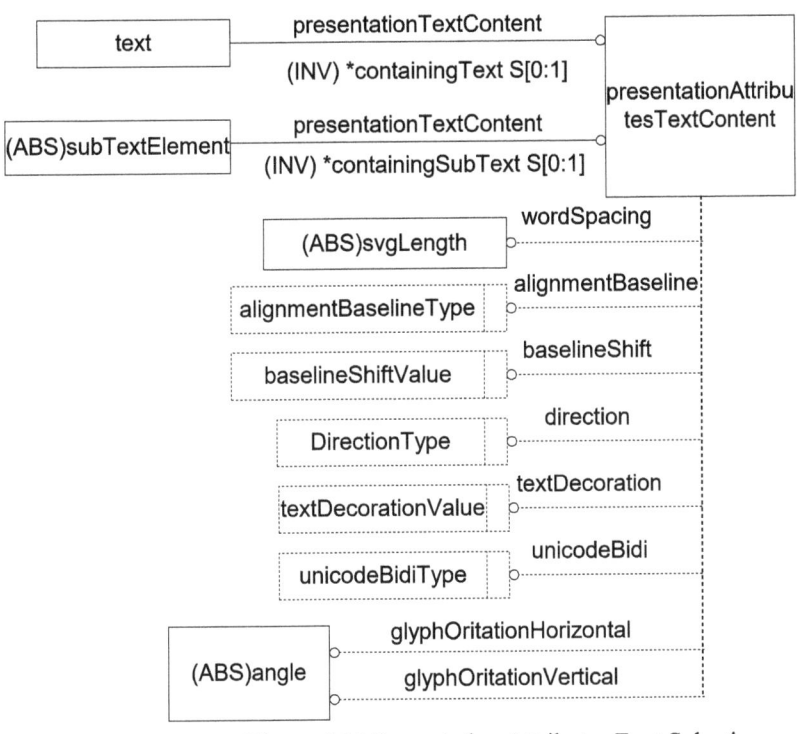

Figure 4.14 Presentation Attributes Font Selection

4.6.6 Text content attributes

The text content attribute (See Figure 4.15) provides the text entity with all its layout attributes such as direction and length.

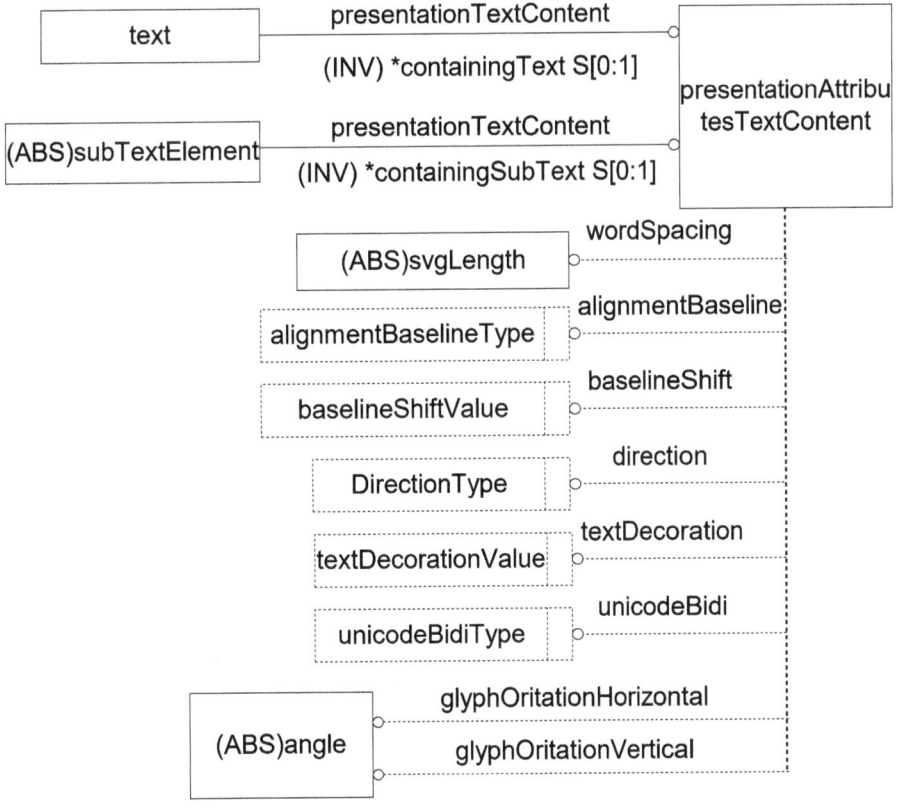

Figure 4.15 Presentation Attributes Text Content

4.6.7 Text attributes

The entity presentationAttributesText (See Figure 4.16) models some extra presentation attributes for `text` entities.

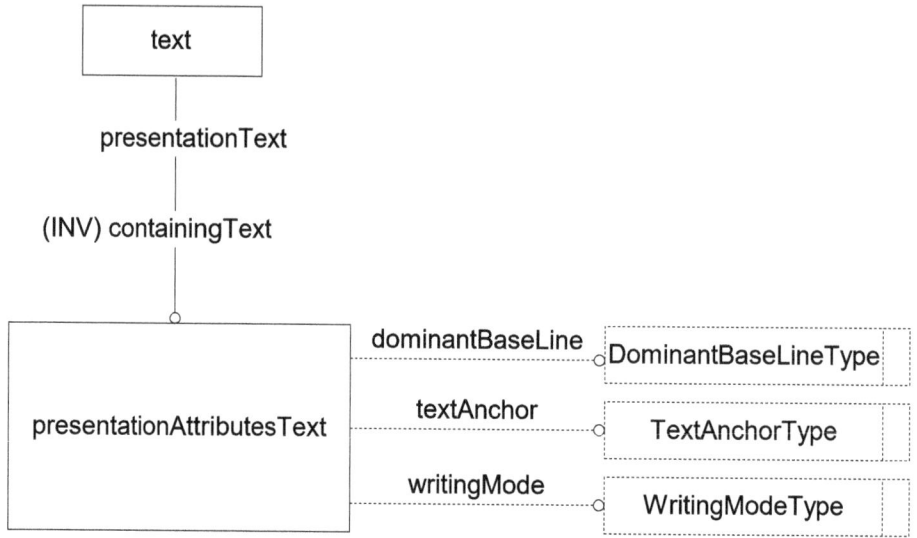

Figure 4.16 Presentation Attributes Text

4.7 Svg_Interactivity_Model

SVG content can be interactive i.e., responsive to user-initiated events. All container entities and graphical entities can be assigned some event entities, attributes of which are scripts, which describe the action when the matching event is triggered.

4.7.1 Script

A `script` entity (See Figure 4.17) is a place for scripts. Any function defined within any script entity has a global scope across the entire document.

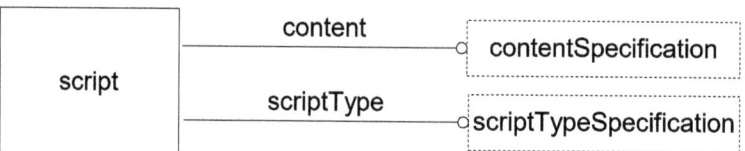

Figure 4.17 Script

4.7.2 Graphic Element Events

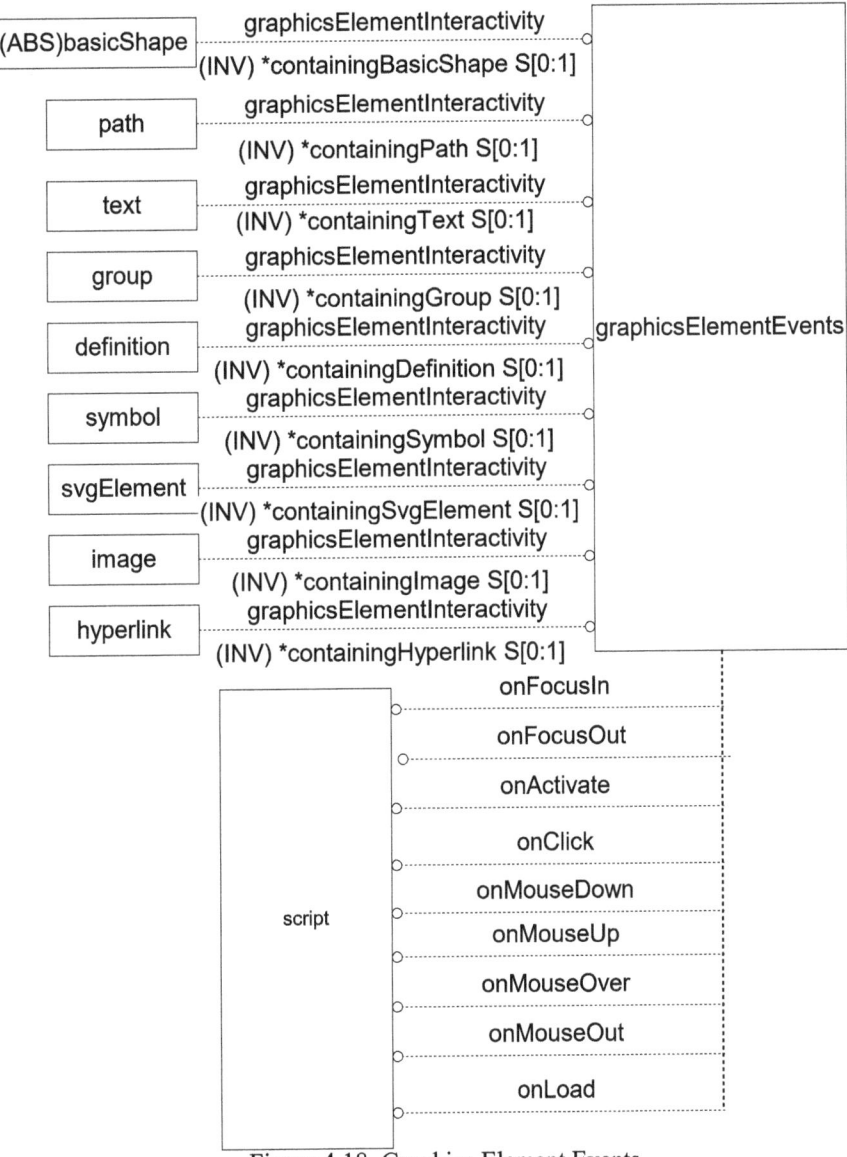

Figure 4.18 Graphics Element Events

The graphicsElementEvents entity (See Figure 4.18) is an assembly of all scripts, which are to be triggered by the graphics entities and container entities.

4.7.3 Document Events

The documentEvents entity (See Figure 4.19) is an assembly of all scripts, which are to be triggered by the document fragment.

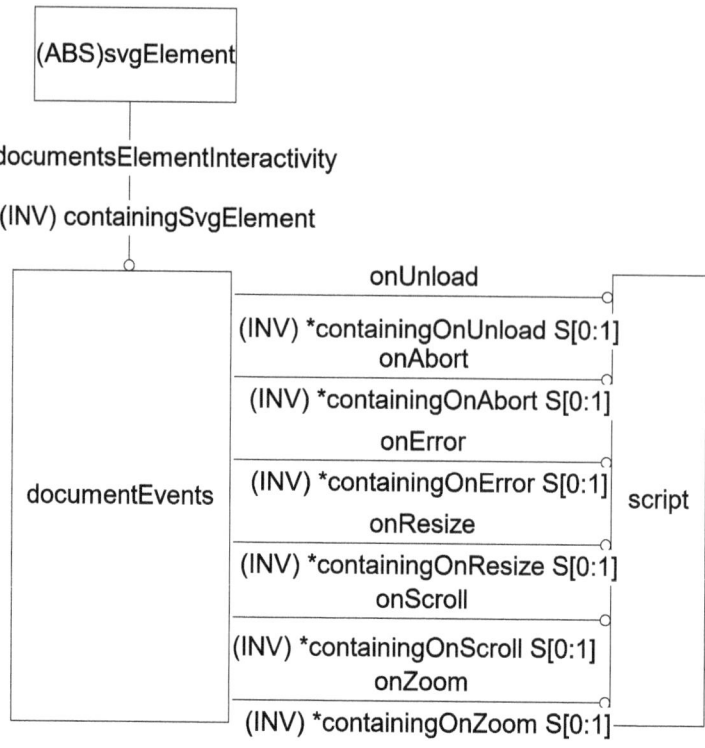

Figure 4.19 Document Elements Events

4.7.4 Animation Events

The `animationEvents` entity (See Figure 4.20) is an assembly of all scripts that are to be triggered by the animations.

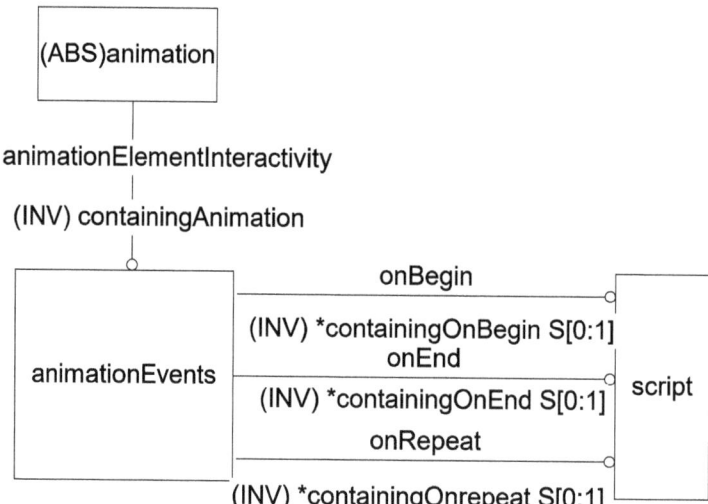

Figure 4.20 Animation Elements Events

4.8 Svg_Animation_Model

Because animation is not relevant to the current research, this schema is incomplete at this time.

4.9 Svg_External_Source_Model

This schema carries some external information. In this context, external has two meanings. The first one is that the definition or data type is not in the domain of SVG, such as CSS or Universal Resource Identification (URI) [W3Cf]. The second one is that the information is necessary to SVG, but not available from the SVG language itself, such as the end user's terminal information.

4.9.1 The terminal user's information

The SVG language is concerned with graphics, so it is very important to represent the data correctly and accurately.

Some of the end user information such as the resolution of the user's monitor is useful when rendering, so it is included in the SVG model and placed in schema `SVG_External_Source_Model`.

4.9.2 Other referenced information

Some other languages are applied in SVG, so parts of their information models are referenced in the SVG model. However, the information models for some of these external languages are not available. Hence it is necessary to give simplified definitions, stubs, of such information in the SVG model in order to satisfy the EXPRESS syntax checking.

The definition of the URI is a good case in point. In the SVG model, a URI is simplified to a string, although its real semantics in its own domain is more complicated.

In summary, the SVG language is a vector 2D graphical language that maintains some compatibility with popular raster-rendering image formats. SVG provides significant support for graphical representation. In the worked examples, it will be treated as a general 2D graphical data format to which the source data are translated.

Chapter 5 Worked example 1: Gerber-To-SVG translator

The research on model based data translation includes two worked examples: a Gerber-To-SVG translator and an AGS-To-SVG translator. In this chapter, the first worked example, the Gerber-To-SVG translator is introduced. The content of this chapter includes an introduction to the Gerber format, an introduction to the Gerber model, the mapping from the Gerber model to the SVG model, and the mapping implementation in Java. The Gerber data format and the SVG language are both in the 2D graphics domain. Hence, in most cases, the translation involves syntactic changes only. However, the mapping will become complicated, when mapping the Gerber entities that do not have semantic equivalents in the SVG model and the information that is implicitly held in the Gerber model.

In this chapter and the following one, which are both about the worked examples, the terms "models" or "information models" mean "information models in EXPRESS". All the models used for the worked examples are written in the EXPRESS language.

5.1 Introduction to the Gerber format

The Gerber Scientific Instrument (GSI) Company defines the Gerber format [Gerber91]. It is a de facto standard language for photoplotting. It has been incorporated within the Electronic Industries Association Recommended Standard EIA RS-274D [EIA80].

The Gerber format offers a simple, generic means of transferring printed circuit board information to a wide variety of devices that convert electronic Printed Circuit Board (PCB) data to artwork produced by a photo plotter. It is a format consisting of X, Y coordinates supplemented by commands that define where the PCB image starts, what shape it will take, and where it ends.

5.1.1 The structure of the Gerber format

A Gerber file is composed of a number of data blocks containing parameters and codes. An example of a Gerber file is given below to show its composition.

```
*G04 EXAMPLE 1:2 BOXES
%FSLAX23Y23*%
%MOIN*%
%OFA0B0*%
%SFA1.0B1.0*%
%ADD10C,0.010*%
%LNBOXES*%
G54D10
X0Y0D01*X5000Y0D01*
X5000Y5000*X0Y5000D01*X0Y0D01*
X6000Y0*X11000Y0D01*
X11000Y5000D01*X6000Y5000D01*
X6000Y5000D01*
```

```
X6000Y0D01*D01*
M02*
```

The basic unit in a Gerber file is the data blocks. Each data block is delimited by an end-of-block character, typically an asterisk (*). Each data block may contain one or more parameters or codes.

One or more data blocks may be grouped into a layer of information that describes part of a graphic image. In the Gerber context, a layer is a named information component of the image composed of one or more data blocks. Each layer may have characteristics, such as a name, a polarity, and an interpolation mode, which differ from other layers' information.

In each data block, some coordinate data and codes specify how the coordinate data should be manipulated. Each code applies to coordinate data located in the same data block, and it applies to coordinate data following it until another code of the same type is encountered, or until a new layer is generated. This continuing action is referred to as modal. There are four categories of codes in Table 5.1: N codes, G codes, D codes and M codes. These are summarized in Table 5.1.

Code	Function	Comments
N	Sequence number	Optional
G	General functions such as linear interpolation, circular interpolation and polygon area fill.	Once encountered, remain in effect until countermanded.
D	Aperture or tool assignment	Once encountered, remain in effect until countermanded.
M	Miscellaneous function: program stop or end.	Every file must end with M00 or M02.

Table 5.1 Gerber Codes

5.1.2 Two coding formats for the Gerber data

The Gerber format can be described and saved using two different formats known as the Word Address Format and the Binary Format. In Word Address Format, Gerber data is described in character coding, of which ASCII is the most widely acceptable form. In Binary Format, Gerber data is described in the form of 16-bit words. The Word Address Format is the more widely accepted one by far, because it has the advantage of being more easily read by humans. The binary format has been little used although it is compact and concise.

A Gerber information model in EXPRESS is already available in the MINT Group, Department of Computer Science, the University of Manchester. It is built on the Word Address Format, but also covers the Binary Format, because these two formats are semantically identical.

5.2 Introduction to the Gerber Model

A Gerber model is defined to capture information about the Gerber format.

The core of the Gerber model is a `gerber_plot` entity (Figure 5.1), which, together with its subcomponents and their own components, represents the structure and the composition of the Gerber format.

5.2.1 The `gerber_plot` entity

In the hierarchy of the Gerber model, the `gerber_plot` entity illustrated in Figure 5.1 is the root, and all other entities are its branches or leaves. A `gerber_plot` entity consists of several `image_layer` entities, as well as some other attributes such as the image name and the image polarity.

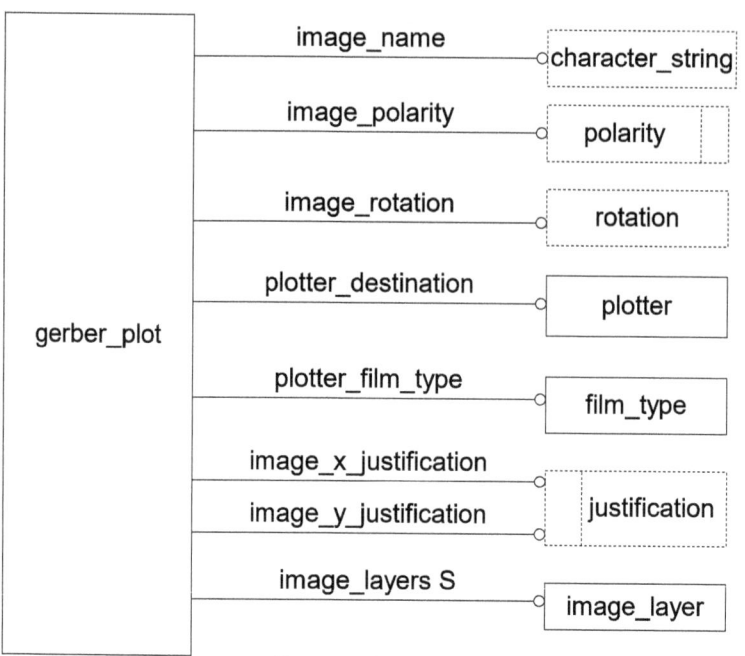

Figure 5.1 Gerber_plot

5.2.2 The `image_layer` entity

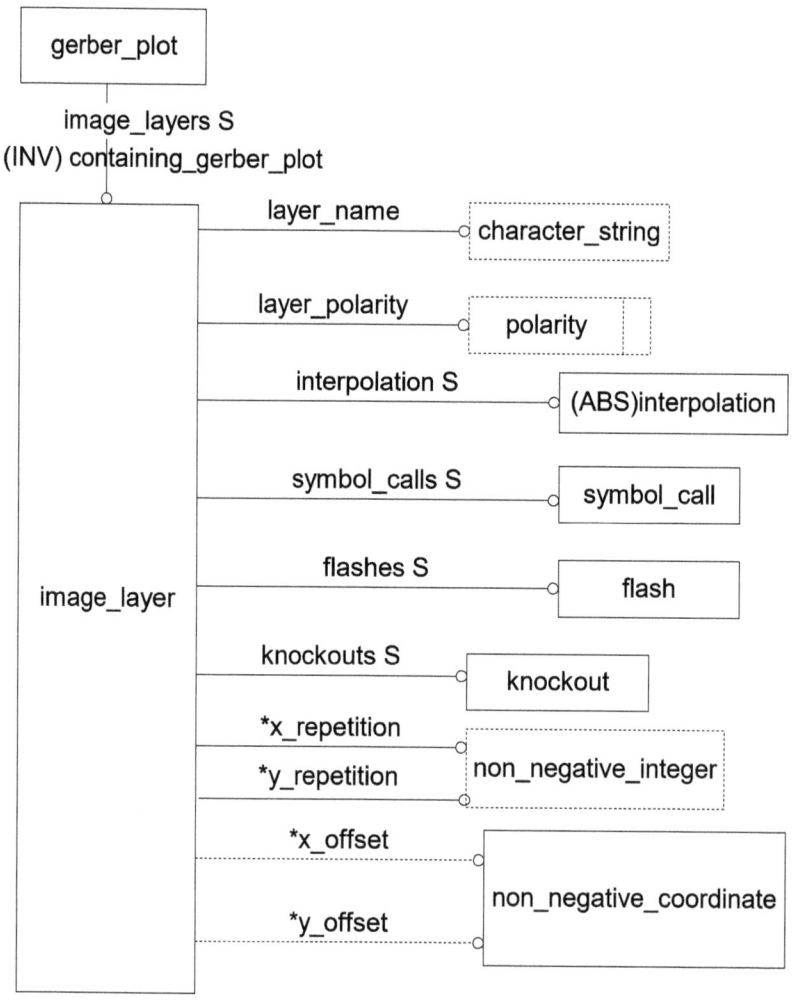

Figure 5.2 Image_layer

A `gerber_plot` entity consists of several layers. An image layer consists of some interpolations of different sorts. This is shown in Figure 5.2.

An `image_layer` entity plays the role of an intermediate level between the outermost `gerber_plot` entity and the entities describing the concrete strokes and movements of the light source through an aperture.

5.2.3 The `interpolation` entity

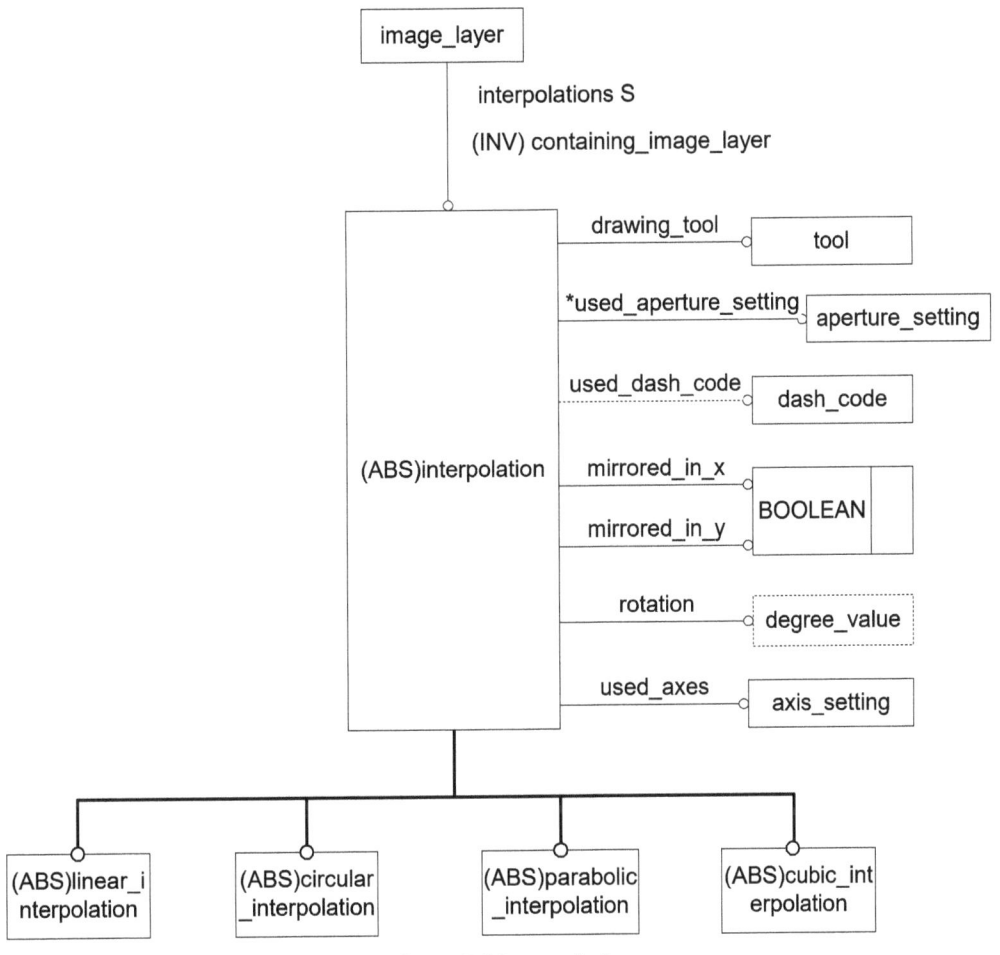

Figure 5.3 Interpolation

An `interpolation` entity represents the result of moving a tool shining a light through a given aperture. It has four subtype entities: `linear_interpolation`, `circular_interpolation`, `parabolic_interpolation`, and `cubic_interpolation`. Each of these is itself a supertype. The four subtypes of `interpolation` (see Figure 5.3) express the four geometric methods of the movements of the light source through an aperture.

5.3 Mapping from the Gerber model to the SVG model

The Gerber-To-SVG translator is based on the mapping from the Gerber model to the SVG model. Both the Gerber model and the SVG model are in the geometry domain, describing some 2D graphic concepts.

There is quite a big overlap between the Gerber model and the SVG model. The entities in the overlap are semantically identical; each pair of them holds the information of the same concept in the geometry world. The mapping between such entities is simple. It only requires some syntactic change.

The mapping will become much more complicated when reaching the part in the Gerber model that cannot find direct correspondents in the SVG model. Some sort of approximation will be used in this mapping.

There is also some implied information in the Gerber. Mapping this information is also complicated. It requires the information to be identified before mapping.

5.3.1 Mapping the overlap of the Gerber model and the SVG model

The SVG language describes two-dimensional graphics. The Gerber format is used to record the movements in two dimensions of the light source through an aperture. This can be regarded as two dimensional geometrical object sequences. For example, a Gerber file that drives the light source to move in straight lines and in circles can be regarded, from the geometrical point of view, as a list of line segments and circles. Hence, the `linear_interpolation` entity in the Gerber model and the `line` entity in the SVG model are semantically identical. There is quite a big overlap between the Gerber model and the SVG model, which covers some basic 2D geometry concepts such as lines, circles and ellipses.

In the overlap of the Gerber model and the SVG model, the mapping involves pairing the semantically equivalent geometrical entities of the source and the target. The pairing is described at the container level in EMM. After the entities are paired, some syntactic changes are defined at the data level. For example, in Figure 5.4 the `linear_interpolation` entity of the Gerber model is mapped to the `line` entity of the SVG model, the `circular_interpolation` entity of the Gerber model is mapped to the

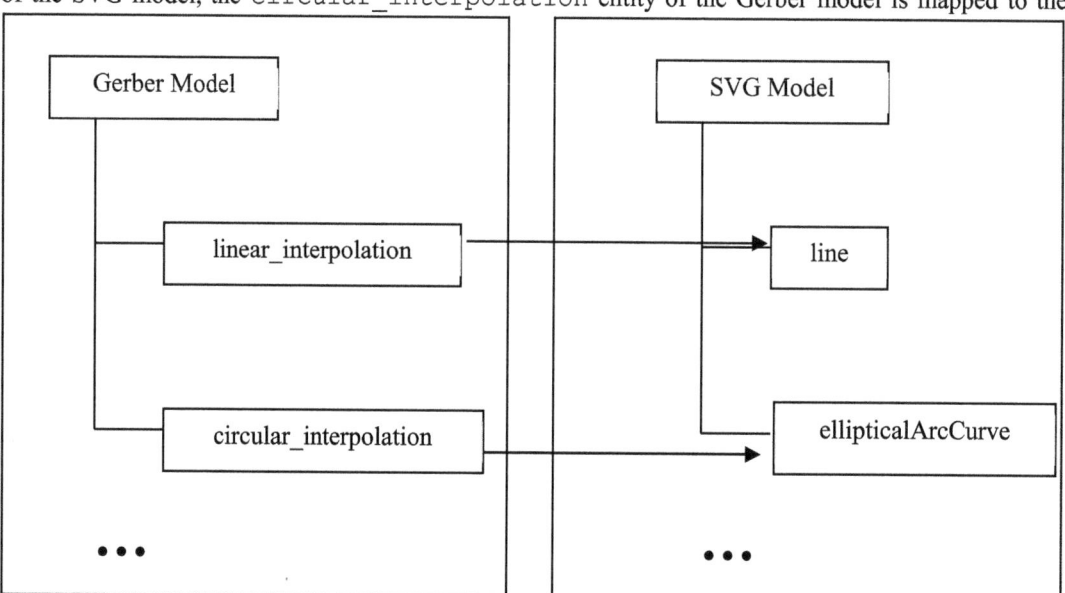

Figure 5.4 Basic Mapping

`ellipticalArcCurve` entity of the SVG model, and so on.

An excerpt from the Gerber model to SVG model mapping description is given below.

```
Mapping Unit ID: Mapping_1
Container level:
Source: Gerber.Gerber_plot;
Target:  SVG.outMostSvgElement.
Data Level:
Source Data Type: entity data type Gerber_plot;
Target Data Type: entity data type outMostSvgElement;
Mapping rule:
```

outMostSvgElement = new outMostSvgElement (Mapping_2(Gerber_plot.image_name)

Mapping_3(Gerber_plot.image_polarity)

Mapping_4(Gerber_plot.image_rotation)).

```
Mapping Unit ID: Mapping_2.
```

Container level:

Source: Gerber.Gerber_plot.image_name;

Target: SVG.outMostSvgElement.etitle.

Data Level:

Source Data Type: defined data type character_string;

Target Data Type: entity data type title.

Mapping rule:

title = new title(eContent = new STRING(character_string)).

Mapping Unit ID: Mapping_3

Container level:

Source: Gerber.Gerber_plot.image_polarity;

Target: SVG.outMostSvgElement.stroke.paintResource;

outMostSvgElement.eBasicShape.

Data level:

Source data type: polarity;

Target data type: squareCornerRectangle, paintResource.

Mapping rule:

outMostSvgElement.eBasic[1] := new squareCorenerRectangle(

boundaryBox(outMostSvgElement).topLeftPoint,

boundaryBox(outMostSvgElement).width,

boundaryBox(outMostSvgElement).height);

if (image_polarity = positive) {

outMostSvgElement.ebasic[1].fill.paintResource = "white";

outMostSvgElement.stroke.paintResource = "black";}

if (image_polarity = negative) {

outMostSvgElement.ebasic[1].fill.paintResource = "black";

outMostSvgElement.stroke.paintResource = "white";}

Mapping Unit ID: Mapping_4.

Container level:

Source: Gerber.Gerber_plot.image_x_justification;

Target: SVG.outMostSvgElement.viewport.leftCorner.x;

Data level:

Source data type: justification;

Target data type: absoluteCoordinate;

Mapping Rule:

if (TYPEOF(image_x_justification) = distance)

outMostSvgElement.viewPort.leftCorner.x = new Coordinate(new svgLength(justification));

if (TYPEOF(image_x_justification)=basic_justification)

if (image_x_justification="left_or_low")

```
outMostSvgElement.viewPort..leftCorner.x = 0;
```

There are four mapping units in the above example, illustrated by Figure 5.5. The dashed lines illustrate the connection between the sources and targets of all mapping units. The `Mapping_1` mapping unit describes the relationship between the `Gerber_plot` entity of the Gerber model and the `outMostSvgElement` entity of the SVG model. The other three mapping units describe the mapping relationships of the attributes of the `Gerber_plot` entity and the `outMostSvgElement` entity.

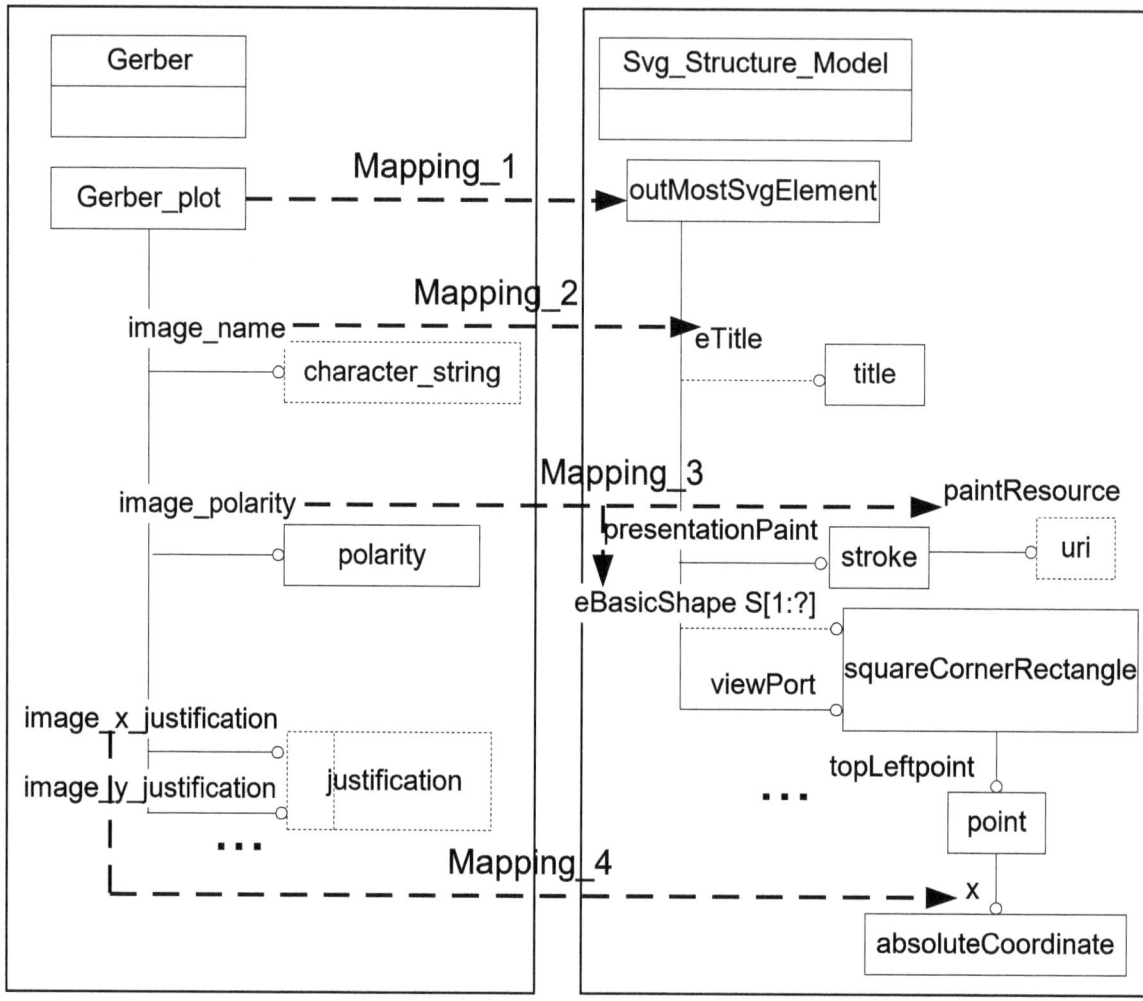

Figure 5.5 Mapping Illustrations

5.3.2 Mapping the part of the Gerber model that is not in SVG model's coverage

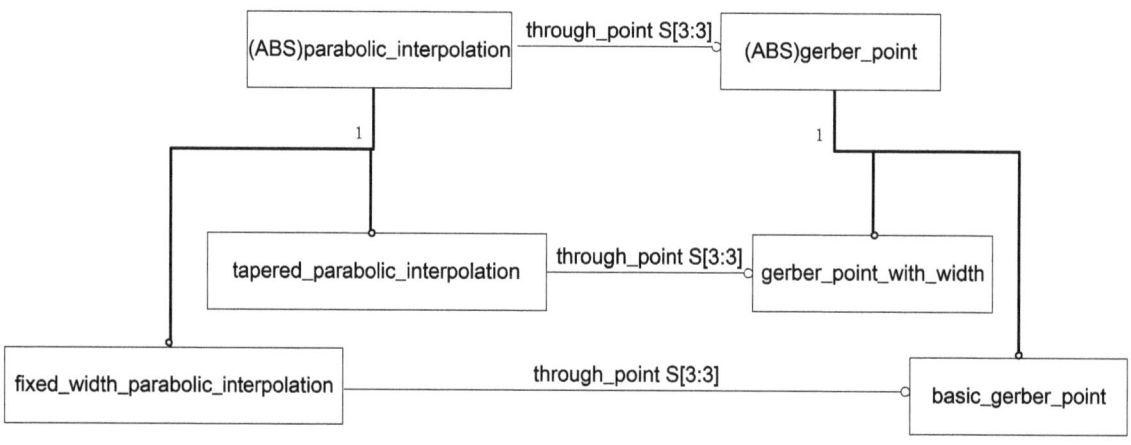

Figure 5.6 The `Parabolic_interpolation` Entity

Now consider the part in the Gerber model that cannot find their correspondents in the SVG model, such as the `parabolic_interpolation` entity that is illustrated in Figure 5.6. Because the SVG model does not cover parabolic curve, the `parabolic_ interpolation` entity does not have a corresponding SVG object that has the same semantics. Then mapping the entities, which hold some information or concept that the SVG model does not cover, is complicated. Such mapping may lead to some approximation. For example, a parabolic interpolation (an instance of the `parabolic_interpolation` entity of the Gerber model) of a Gerber file will be approximated by a string of connected lines (some instances of the `line` entity of the SVG model) of an SVG file. On the data level, a parabolic interpolation in a Gerber file is mapped to some lines that are connected one by one in an SVG file; on the container level, the `parabolic_interpolation` entity of the Gerber model is mapped to the `line` entity of the SVG model. The following part is the specification in EMM.

```
Mapping Unit ID: Mapping_17;
Container level:
    Source:Gerber.fixed_width_parabolic_interpolation;
    Target:SVG.line;
Data level:
    Source Data Type: fixed_width_parabolic_interpolation;
    Target Data Type: line [];
Mapping Rules:
    Line [] Target = new Array [] line;
    Target           =           fixed_width_parabolic_interpolation.
transformToLines(approximationPrecision);
```

In the `Mapping_17` mapping unit, a `fixed_width_parabolic_interpolation` entity instance is mapped to an array of `line` entity instances. The `transformToLines` method defines the approximation algorithm in detail, and the `approximationPrecision` parameter passes the necessary approximation precision specification.

The mapping requires much help of the configuration and functions to implement the approximation. The configuration should set down the approximation algorithm and some parameters such as the approximation precision. In the above example of the `parabolic_interpolation` entity in the Gerber model, it may be mapped to some other entities in the SVG model such as the `ellipticalArcCurve` entity and the `connectedLineSegment` entity, because they are capable of approximating the parabolic curve too. The configuration should also set down some parameters such as the approximation precision that are important to complete the approximation. Because of the manual implementation, the configuration has not been formally specified. The following research will include configuration, such as the formal configuration specification and configuration pluggability to the mapping specifications.

5.3.3 Mapping the implied information in the Gerber model

Though the Gerber model and the SVG model are in the same domain, they are at different levels. The Gerber model is at a lower level.

For example, although the Gerber format does not include the high level concepts of circle, rectangle and polygon as well as the low level concepts such as linear interpolation and circular interpolation, it is able to express these geometric concepts in other ways. For example, the Gerber format can express a circle by filling its inside space with many parallel line segments (See Figure 5.7 A). In other words, circles are implied in the Gerber files

On the other hand, the SVG model is able to express a circle by its centre and its radius (See Figure 5.7

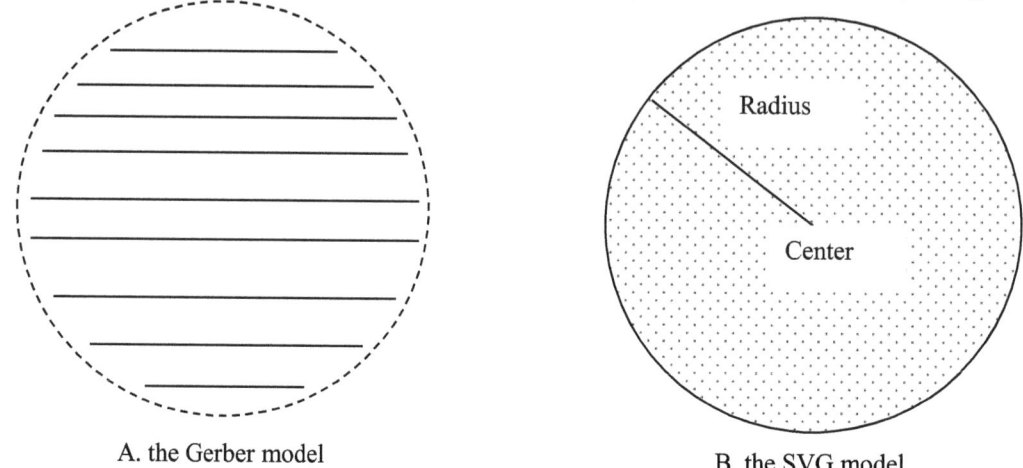

A. the Gerber model   B. the SVG model

Figure 5.7 A Circle at Different Conceptual Levels

B), in the normal way. The Gerber model and the SVG model represent some geometric elements such as circles at different conceptual levels. The Gerber model is at a low level, whereas the SVG model is at a higher one. Mapping in such cases should be able to relate the source and the target that are not at the same conceptual level, This is a more complicated process than a mapping carried out between objects at the same conceptual level. For the example in Figure 5.7, the mapping from the hundreds of lines in the Gerber model to a circle in the SVG model is quite difficult to define and formally describe. In order to pass over as much semantics as possible and improve the mapping efficiency, it is necessary to focus on the implied information, dig it out and pass it to the target model. Mapping between circles has not been specified in EMM so far. The difficulties lie in identifying the lines that compose the circle as opposed to other lines. Some more advanced semantics analysis tools are needed to address this issue.

5.4 Mapping implementation in Java

This step checks the correctness of the above simple mapping. It is a manually created implementation based on the EMM mapping. The architecture of the Gerber-to-SVG translator is given in Figure 5.8.

5.4.1 The structure of the Gerber-To-SVG translator

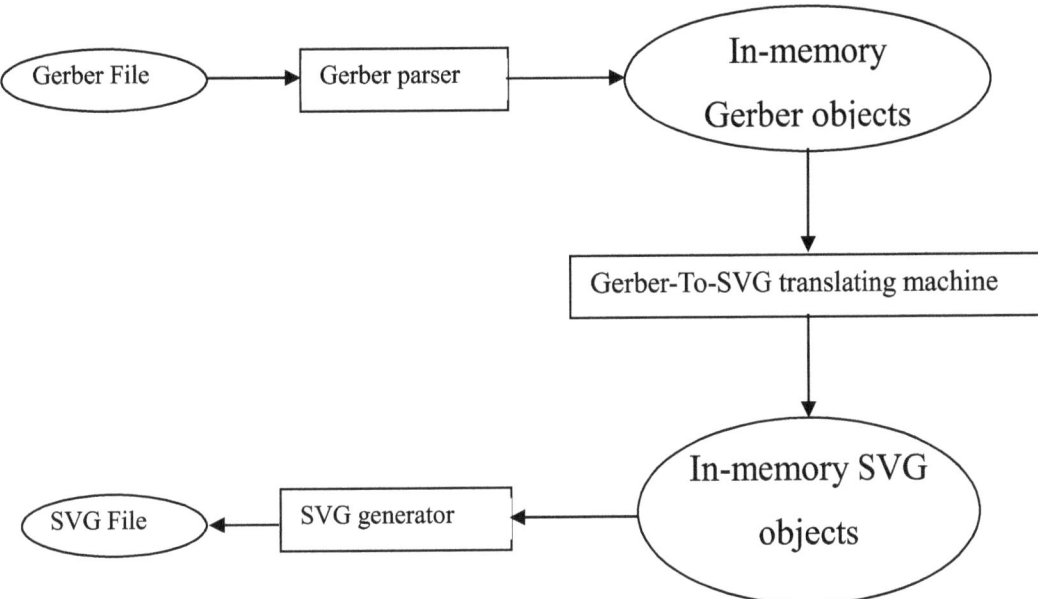

Figure 5.8 The Structure of the Gerber-To-SVG Translator

The Gerber-To-SVG translator consists of three modules, the Gerber parser, the translating machine and the SVG generator (See Figure 5.8).

The Gerber file parser parses the input Gerber file and builds Gerber objects in memory. The in-memory Gerber objects are compliant with the Java classes that are implemented from the Gerber information model. It was created with JavaCC [WEBGAIN].

The Gerber-To-SVG translating machine scans the in-memory Gerber objects; identifies the objects that match the mapping source specifications (at both the container level and the data level), and then generates some SVG objects according to the identified Gerber objects.

The SVG file generator scans the in-memory SVG objects and generates the corresponding SVG fragment. XML technologies such as Document Object Model (DOM) [W3Cd] have been applied during this step.

The Gerber-To-SVG translating machine is the core of the translator. It is the implementation of the

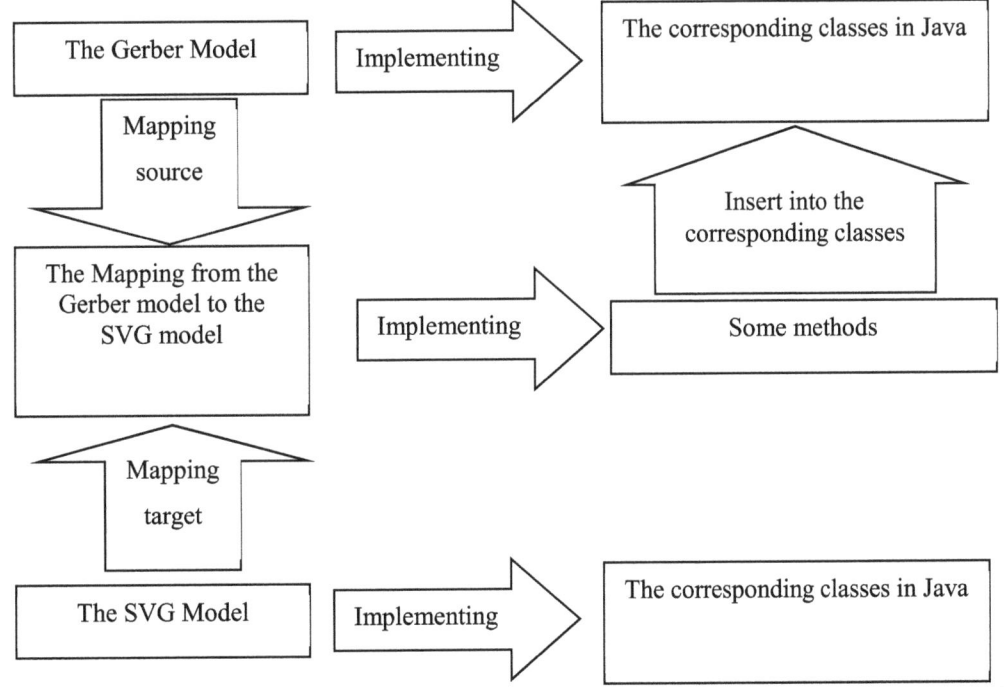

Figure 5.9 Mapping Implementation

mapping from the Gerber model to the SVG model.5.4.2 implementing the mapping specification

Figure 5.9 shows that some Java classes are generated from both the Gerber model and the SVG model. Some methods in Java are also generated from the mapping specification and inserted into the classes generated from the Gerber model.

There are various units in the mapping specification. Figure 5.10 shows the implementation of a single mapping unit. A method will be generated from a mapping unit. The signature of a method includes the method name, the method parameter and the method return data type. The method name will be captured from the mapping unit's identification. The method parameters are copied from the data types of the source of the mapping unit, and the method's return data type is copied from the data type of the target. The method body is an integration of the mapping rules and the contents of the container level.

Finally, a Gerber-to-SVG translator, which is qualified to do its job, is produced.

5.4.3 Example of jobs done by the Gerber-To-SVG translator

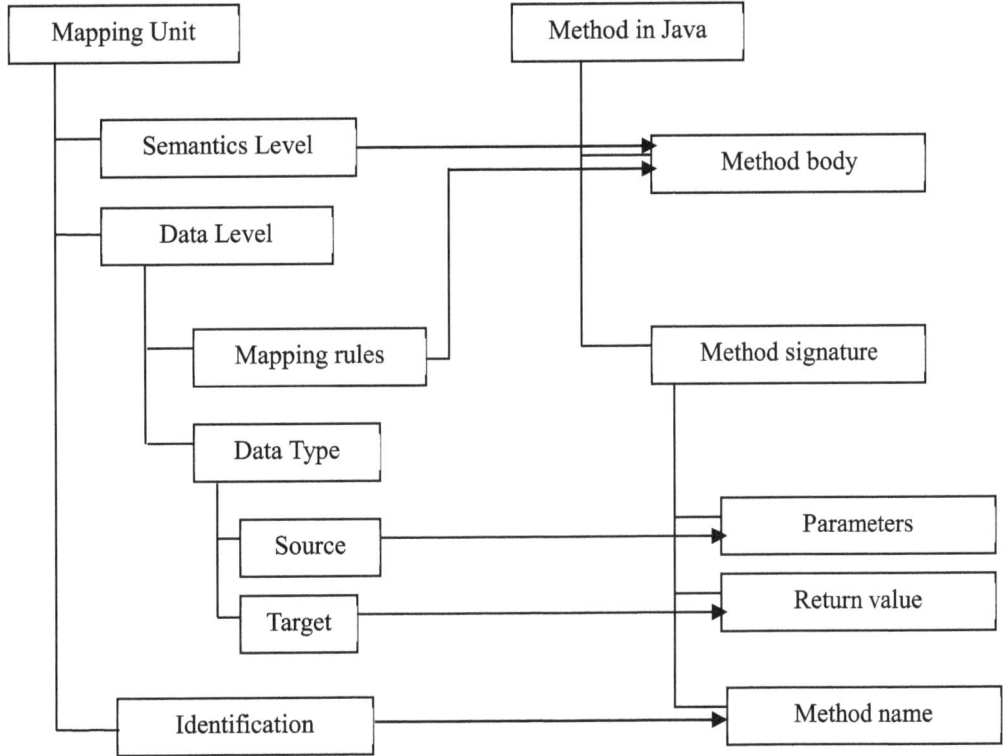

Figure 5.10 Mapping Unit Implementation

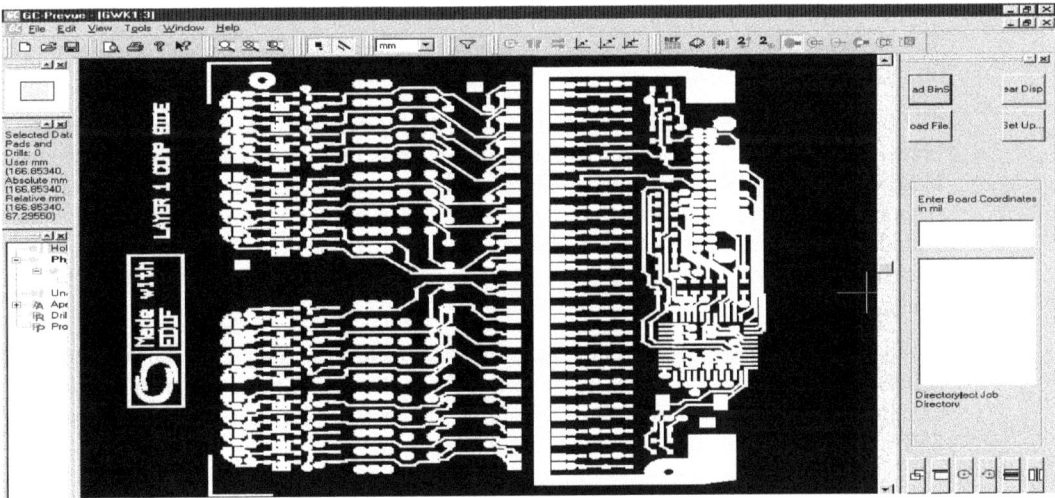

Figure 5.11 Example Gerber Data   (Viewed by GCPrevue)

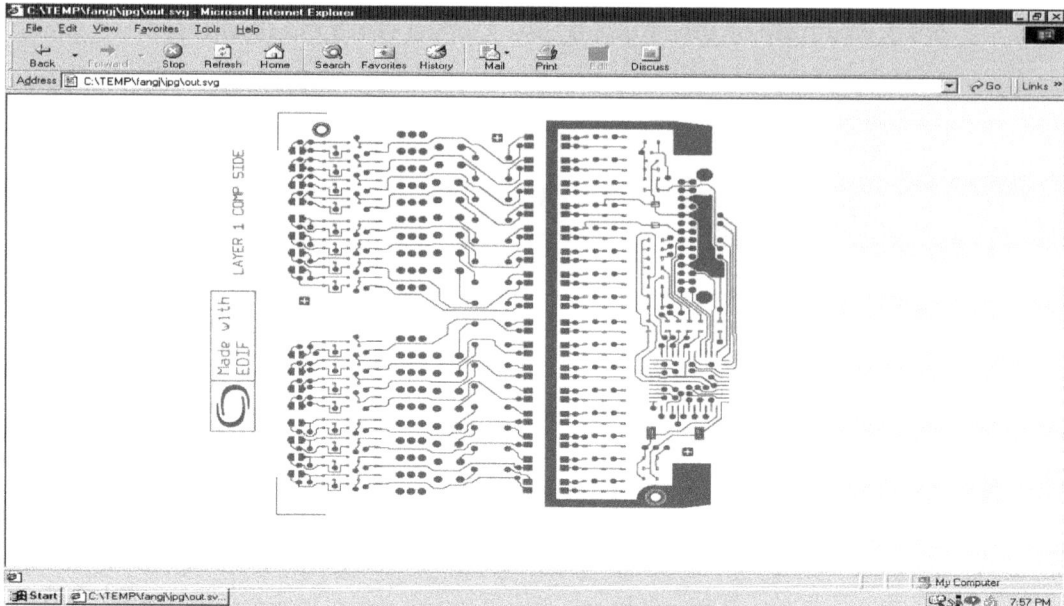

Figure 5.12 Translated SVG Data (Viewed with Adobe SVG viewer)

The figures above illustrate an example of the results produced by the translator. In Figure 5.11, a Gerber file, which is taken from the Gertrude Project [Gertrude], is viewed using GCPrevue, a conventional Gerber viewer supplied by Graphicode [Graphicode], and in Figure 5.12, the SVG file generated by the translator is viewed using Adobe SVG viewer [ASV], a plug-in to Internet Explorer [IE]. Both the image colors and the background colours in Figure 5.11 and 5.12 are different. They are the default colors of GCPrevue and the Adobe SVG viewer respectively.

5.5 Conclusions

The Gerber model is mapped to the SVG model, and a Gerber-To-SVG data translator is created based on this mapping. The mapping is the core of the data translator development.

The Gerber model and the SVG model are in a same domain, but have different coverage. The mapping between them ranges from simple to complicated. The simple part only requires some syntactic change. However, the complicated part, when mapping the source entities that are not in the target coverage and mapping some implied information, has identified the need for some sophisticated approach perhaps including even some intermediate models. How to generate the configuration, auxiliary functions and the intermediate models, and how to pursue the best solution according to the concrete case are worthy studying.

In this Chapter, a Gerber-To-SVG translator is created. Both the source and the target are graphics-related and therefore the mapping involves relating objects that are expected to map reasonably well. Some example data files that are from the Gertrude Project are used to test the correctness of the Gerber-To-SVG translator. One of the tests is illustrated in Section 5.4.3.

In the next chapter, a translator, using a source that is non-graphics related and a graphics-related target will be introduced.

Chapter 6 Worked example 2: AGS-To-SVG translator

This chapter considers the second worked example of model based data translation, and addresses the issue of translating non-graphics-related files to graphics files (the SVG files in this book).

The content of this chapter includes an introduction to the AGS format [AGS99], an introduction to the AGS model, the mapping from the AGS model to the SVG model, and the mapping implementation in Java.

Since the whole procedure of developing a model based data translator has already been introduced in Chapter 5, this chapter focuses on the issue of the mapping between the non-graphics-related model (the AGS model) and the graphics model (the SVG model), which is different from the case study in Chapter 5.

6.1 Introduction to the AGS format

Computer based technology is gradually becoming accepted as part of the support environment in the geotechnical industry. The producers of geotechnical data have adopted a data representation system to support the efficient storage, exchange, preparation and presentation of reports. Clearly, the electronically transfer of data without the need for a printed interface helps to minimize costs, time and the potential for error. It also encourages better use of the data.

Prior to the establishment of the AGS Format, which has now been widely accepted by the geotechnical community, there was a proliferation of software systems that differed in both form and purpose even though much of their content was common. This was recognized by AGS in 1991 and led to the setting up of a Working Party to establish an interchange format that allowed transfer of data between systems with minimum change to the systems themselves. The outcome of this work was the AGS Interchange Format.

6.1.1 The composition of the AGS Format

The AGS Format file is a text file, containing groups of information on many aspects of geotechnical site investigation.

The AGS format is a variant of a conventional comma separated format. Commas are used to separate the members of the lists of items. An AGS file consists of some groups, each of which is identified by a group name preceded by two asterisks (**).   In each group of data in an AGS file, the lists of values are preceded by a string of data headings, a record that is the list of tags (also comma separated). Headings preceded by one asterisk (*).

Here is an excerpt from an example AGS format file.

```
"**PROJ"

"*PROJ_ID","*PROJ_NAME","*PROJ_LOC","*PROJ_CLNT","*PROJ_ENG","*PROJ_C
ONT","*PROJ_DATE","*PROJ_AGS","FILE_FSET"
"<UNITS>","","","","","","dd/mm/yyyy","",""

"7845","Trumpington    Sewerage","Trumpington","Trumpington    District
Council","Geo-Knowledge    International","Lithosphere    Investigations
Ltd","23/07/1999","3","FS0001"
```

```
"**HOLE"

"*HOLE_ID","*HOLE_TYPE","*HOLE_NATE","*HOLE_NATN","*HOLE_GL","*HOLE_F
DEP","*HOLE_STAR","*HOLE_LOG","FILE_FSET"
"<UNITS>","","m","m","m","m","dd/mm/yyyy","",""

"TP501","TP","523196","178231","61.86","3.25","21/07/1999","ANO","FS0
02"

"BH502","IP+CP","523142","178183","58.72","15.45","22/07/1999","ANO",
"FS003"


"**GEOL"

"*HOLE_ID","*GEOL_TOP","*GEOL_BASE","*GEOL_DESC","*GEOL_LEG","*GEOL_G
EOL","*GEOL_STAT","FILE_FSET"

"<UNITS>","m","m","","","","",""

"TP501","0.00","0.25","Friable brown sandy CLAY with numerous rootlets
(Topsoil)","101","TS","A",""

"TP501","0.25","1.55","Firm brown slightly sandy very closely fissured
CLAY with some fine to coarse subrounded gravel. Medium spaced
subhorizontal slightly polished gleyed shear surfaces. Widely spaced
vertical rough desiccat","","","",""

"<CONT>","","","ion cracks with concentrations of rootlets. (Weathered
Boulder Clay)","261","WBC","B",""

"TP501","1.55","3.25","Stiff grey closely fissured CLAY with a little
fine to medium subrounded gravel and rare sandstone cobbles (Boulder
Clay)","250","BC","C",""

"BH502","0.00","0.30","Friable brown sandy CLAY with numerous rootlets
(Topsoil)","101","TS","",""

"BH502","0.30","2.60","Firm brown very closely fissured CLAY with a
little fine to medium subrounded gravel (Weathered Boulder
Clay)","250","WBC","",""   "BH502","2.60","5.75","Stiff grey slightly
sandy closely fissured CLAY with some fine to coarse subrounded gravel
(Boulder    Clay)","261","BC","",""      "BH502","5.75","15.45","Dense
becoming very dense yellow brown very sandy fine to coarse subrounded
GRAVEL (Glacial Gravels)","307","GG","",""


"**SAMP"

"*HOLE_ID","*SAMP_TOP","*SAMP_REF","*SAMP_TYPE","*SAMP_BASE","*SAMP_D
ATE","*SAMP_TIME""*GEOL_STAT","FILE_FSET"
"<UNITS>","m","","","m","dd/mm/yyyy","hhmmss","",""

"TP501","1.00","1","D","1.00","","","B",""

"TP501","1.00","2","B","1.30","","","B",""

"TP501","2.50","3","B","2.75","","","C",""
"BH502","1.00","1","U","1.45","","","","FS058"
"BH502","1.50","2","D","1.50","","","",""

"BH502","3.00","3","U","3.45","","","",""

"BH502","3.50","4","D","3.50","","","",""

"BH502","6.00","5","D","6.45","","","",""

"BH502","6.00","6","B","6.50","","","",""

"BH502","9.00","7","D","9.45","","","",""

"BH502","9.00","8","B","9.50","","","",""
```

```
"BH502","10.00","9","B","10.50","","","",""
"BH502","12.00","10","B","12.50","","","",""
"BH502","3.00","11","W","3.00","22/07/1999","120000","",""
"BH502","3.00","12","W","3.00","22/07/1999","153000","",""
```

In the above AGS file excerpt, there are four groups: PROJ, HOLE, GEOL and SAMP. Each group comprises a group name, a list of field headings, a list of units and some data. The PROJ group has a name PROJ, which is preceded by two asterisks. It has a list of field headings, each of which is preceded by an asterisk. There are two lists of values in the group, one is for the unit definitions, and another one contains some data.

6.1.2 Groups

Generally, in order to compose the data in a consistent and logical manner, an AGS format file is divided into data groups, within which series of fields are defined. The data groups have been chosen to relate to specific elements for which data are obtained, such as project information, exploratory hole details and strata details. For data of a more complex nature, two or more linked data groups are defined.

It is necessary to have a closer look at the composition of a group. Table 6.1 illustrates the HOLE group in the above AGS file excerpt.

Group Name	HOLE								
Field Heading	HOLE_ID (*)	HOLE_TYPE	HOLE_NATE	HOLE_NATN	HOLE_GL	HOLE_FDEP	HOLE_STAR	HOLE_LOG	FILE_FSET
UNITS		-	m	m	m	m	dd/mm/yyyy	-	-
Record 1	TP501	TP	523196	178231	61.86	3.25	21/07/99	ANO	FS002
Record 2	BH502	IP+CP	523141	178183	58.72	15.45	22/07/99	ANO	FS003

(Note: the field heading marked with an asterisk is a key.)

Table 6.1 Structure of HOLE Group

This group has a name HOLE, nine field headings, and five units. There is a rule that the HOLE_ID field never has a unit. The units are unnecessary for HOLE_TYPE, HOLE_LOG and HOLE_FSET fields. The group also includes two data records each of which consists of nine data entries.

Fields within each data group identify specific items such as stratum description or sample depth. Each field has a status that can be either KEY or COMMON.

In the HOLE group, there are nine fields: HOLE_ID (*), HOLE_TYPE, HOLE_NATE, HOLE_NATN, HOLE_GL, HOLE_FDEP, HOLE_STAR, HOLE_LOG, FILE_FSET. The HOLE_ID is the key field, and the others are common. Key fields are necessary in order to define the data unambiguously. The common data fields contain the associated data.

6.1.3 The hierarchical structure of the AGS Format

6.1.3.1 The hierarchical structure

In the AGS format, the data groups are organized in a hierarchy. At the root of the hierarchy is the Hole group, and all other groups lie below it. One of the groups immediately below Hole is Samp; all the laboratory-testing groups lie below Samp. Hole is termed the parent group of Samp. Each group has only one parent, but there can be many groups below each parent. Equally, each group is linked to the groups below it by key fields. For this structure to work, and the link to be made correctly between related groups, the data in the key fields must be consistent and unique. If a data group is included in an AGS file, its parent group must also be included. The key fields play a very important role in maintaining the hierarchy.

6.1.3.2 The stand-alone groups

Six groups are not part of the hierarchical structure. The `PROJ`, `ABBR`, `CODE`, `DICT`, `FILE` and `UNIT` groups are separated from the hierarchy. Each has a specific purpose. The `PROJ`, `ABBR` and `UNIT` groups must always be included in an AGS format file as they define the project, the abbreviations and the units within the groups. The `CODE` group must be included if the `CNMT` group is used for chemical test results, as the `CODE` group defines the codes used within `CNMT`. The `DICT` group must be included if any user defined groups or fields are present. The `FILE` group must be included if any associated files (non-AGS format files) are introduced in the AGS format file.

Figure 6.1 illustrates the hierarchy of the example excerpt: The `HOLE` group is the parent of both `GEOL` and `SAMP` groups, and the `PROJ` group is stand-alone.

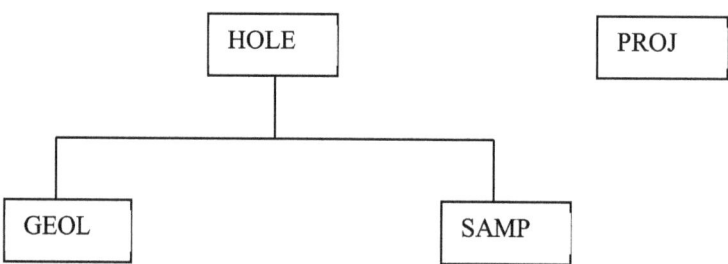

Figure 6.1 Hierarchy of an Example AGS File

6.2 Introduction to the AGS Model

An AGS model that captures the above information and concepts is available in the MINT group, University of Manchester. The AGS format, in effect, is a description of the metadata of a database in a text form. The metadata includes the definition of tables (called groups in the AGS context), the data types of fields (called units in the AGS context), and the hierarchical structure of the tables that is maintained by the key fields. Modelling the AGS format means representing the metadata in the EXPRESS language. In order to model the table definitions, all groups in the AGS format will be transformed to some EXPRESS entities, and their fields will be transformed to some attributes. Thus, there is a one-to-one relationship between the groups in the AGS format and the entities in the AGS model. The hierarchy in the AGS format is copied into the AGS model too.

6.2.1 Modelling the groups

Each of the groups in the AGS format has a corresponding entity in the AGS model. For example, the `HDIA` group in Table 6.2 was represented by a `hole_diameter_by_depth` entity (see Figure 6.2) in the AGS model. The `HDIA` group has three fields, `HOLE_ID`, `HDIA_HDEP`, and `HDIA_HOLE`, which is a key. The corresponding entity `hole_diameter_by_depth` has two common attributes, `depth_achived` that expresses `HDIA_HDEP`, and `borehole_diameter` that expresses `HDIA_HOLE`. The data types of the `depth_achived` and `borehole-diameter` attributes follow the unit specification in the `HDIA` group.

Group Name: HDIA - Hole Diameter by Depth				
Status	Heading	Unit	Description	Example
*	HOLE_ID		Exploratory hole or traverse name/number	6421/A
	HDIA_HDEP	m	Depth achieved at HDIA_HOLE	18
	HDIA_HOLE	mm	Borehole diameter	200

Table 6.2 Structure of HDIA Group

The correspondent of the key field `HOLE_ID` of the `HDIA` group is the INVERSE attribute `containing_hole`. This INVERSE attribute may receive a `hole` entity, whose `hole_diameter_by_depths` attribute references this `hole_diameter_by_depth` entity.

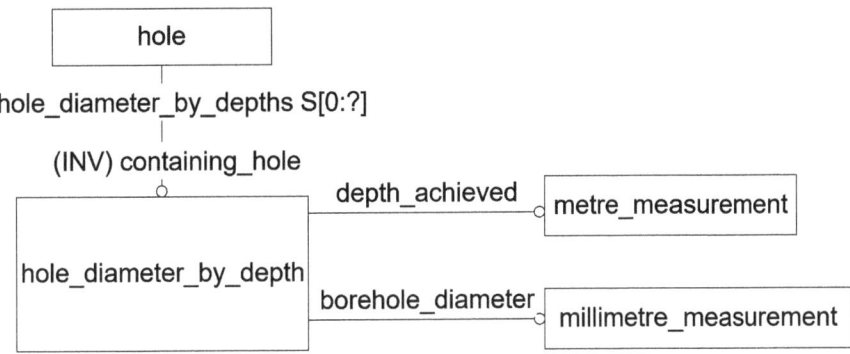

Figure 6.2 Model of HDIA Group

6.2.2 Modelling the hierarchy structure

All AGS groups are organized in a tree-like hierarchical structure. Modelling the AGS format should also cover its hierarchical structure. Since all the groups in the AGS format have their correspondents in the AGS model, it is possible to construct the hierarchy among the entities in the AGS model that is a copy of the one of the AGS format. The hierarchy in the AGS format is constructed on the base of the key fields that link the master groups and the slave ones, while the hierarchy in the AGS model is based on the INVERSE attributes that establish the existence dependence.

Consider the `HDIA` group in Table 6.2 and its corresponding `hole_diameter_by_depth` entity in Figure 6.2. The `HDIA` group is a child of the `HOLE` group, and the link between them is the `HOLE_ID` attribute that they share, while the `hole_diameter_by_depth` entity is dependent on the `hole` entity, and this existence dependence is maintained by the `hole_diameter_by_depths` attribute of the `hole` entity and the `containing_hole` INVERSE attribute of the `hole_diameter_by_depth` entity.

6.3 Mapping from the AGS model to the SVG model

The AGS-To-SVG translator is based on the mapping from the AGS model to the SVG model. The AGS model and the SVG model are in different domains; the AGS model is in the geotechnical and geoenvironmental domain; whereas the SVG model is in the graphics domain. An entity in the AGS model cannot find a semantic equivalent in the SVG model. The mapping between these two models involves much more than syntactic changes alone.

6.3.1 Comparing with the mapping between the Gerber model and the SVG model

The Gerber model (introduced in Chapter 5) and the SVG model are both 2D-graphics-related. They have a big overlap. The mapping from the Gerber model to the SVG model, in many cases, involves finding the appropriate equivalences and applying some syntactic changes to them. For example, in Figure 5.4, the `linear_interpolation` entity in the Gerber model and the `line` entity in the SVG model are semantically equivalent. Hence, it is reasonable to map the Gerber `linear_interpolation` entity to the SVG `line` entity. Mapping the `linear_interpolation` entity to the `circle` entity in the SVG model is absurd to all programmers who have any basic graphical knowledge. In other words, the container level specification of the mapping from the Gerber model to the SVG model is unambiguous because of the semantic overlap between them.

However, the mapping from the AGS model to the SVG model is much more ambiguous because it has a non-graphics-related source and a graphics-related target. The source and the target of the mapping are heterogeneous. The AGS model has various entities, and they all are about geotechnical and geoenvironmental technologies. Moreover, the AGS model is composed as a representation of database metadata, not for graphical presentations. Thus, the AGS model is semantically far away from the SVG model. The mapping from the AGS model to the SVG model, which is for representing the geotechnical and geoenvironmental data graphically in the SVG language, shall cover the great distance between these two models.

6.3.2 Mapping issues to be addressed

The mapping from the AGS model to the SVG model is complicated and requires more than syntactic changes. Various issues need to be addressed.

6.3.2.1 Mapping source

The first issue is what information in the AGS model is to be mapped. In other words, what entities in the AGS model need mapping? The target of the AGS-To-SVG translator is the geotechnical and geoenvironmental data graphical representation. The AGS model is related to drilling investigation, including the location of the excavation, the shape of the hole or traverse, all sorts of chemical and physical tests on the core, and so on. Theoretically, all information may be graphically illustrated. In this work, only part of the AGS model is mapped, considering the necessity and the cost. The exact mapping source is dependent on the user's motivation and requirements, and is variable.

The AGS-To-SVG translator in this book focuses on the geometry-related information in the AGS model, such as the location and shape of the holes or traverse. Therefore, the geometry-related entities and attributes are selected and mapped to the SVG model; the other entities and attributes are ignored. For example, the `hole` entity in the AGS model contains some hole location and depth information, that is geometry-related and is therefore mapped. The `hole` entity has many attributes, such as the local grid coordinate, the hole type, final depth of hole and the date of start of excavation. The `hole` entity is mapped in order to represent its location and shape. Hence, only the attributes that are related to local grid coordinates and depth are to be mapped; the other attributes are ignored.

If the mapping is for some other purpose, then some other entities and attributes will be selected and mapped. For example, if the mapping purpose is to illustrate the drilling process of the hole, then the `hole_end_date` attribute of the `hole` entity that is about the hole end date will be mapped to a graphical illustration.

6.3.2.2 Mapping target

The second issue, once the mapping source is determined, is what the mapping target is. What entity in the SVG model should the `hole` entity in the AGS model be mapped to? The mapping is to graphically represent the location of hole; the most common way is to draw some symbols, each of which stands for a hole, according to the coordinates of the hole. An example is shown in Figure 6.6. The symbol for a hole may be varied. In this case, a circle or a square is selected. As a result, the `hole` entity may be mapped to the `circle` or the `rectangle` entity of the SVG model.

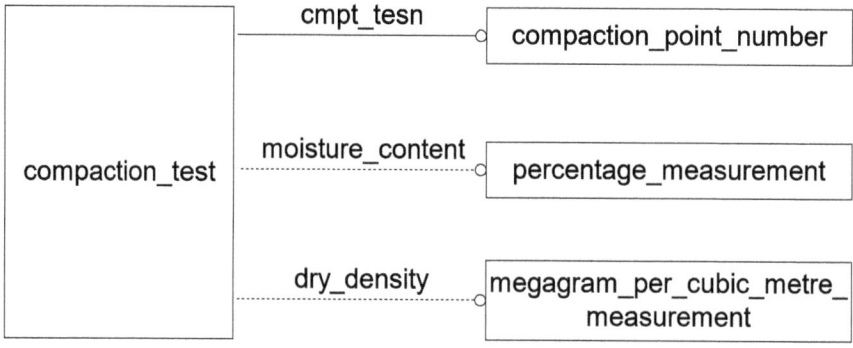

Figure 6.3 The `Compaction_test` Entity

Point number	10551	10552	10553	10554
Moisture content	20.4	27.4	90	20.4
Dry density	30.6	38.6	34.6	31.6

Table 6.3 Data Example

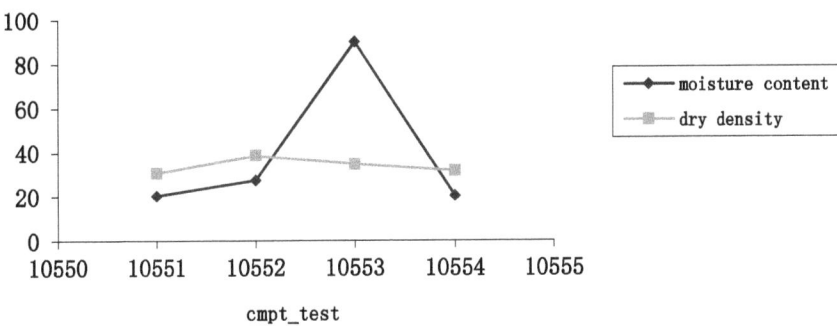

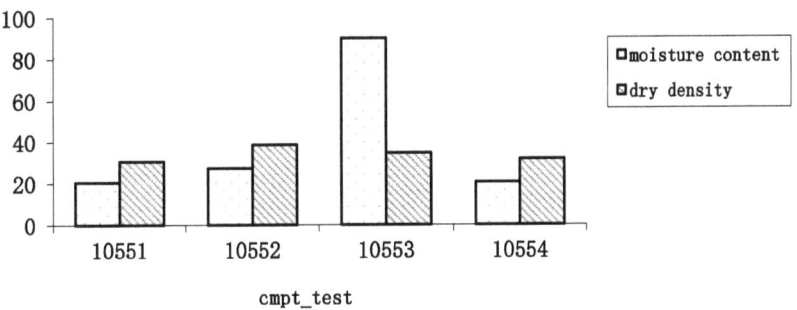

Figure 6.5 Different Representations for the Same Data

Above is another example for a single entity in the AGS model that may be graphically represented using different approaches. Given the `compaction_test` entity, summarized in Figure 6.3, in the AGS model, the moisture content and the dry density can be illustrated in many ways (see Figure 6.4 and Table 6.3). Figure 6.4 offers two possible presentations. The compact_test_representation_1 diagram presents the data in Table 6.3 in the form of a graph constructed from lines, text, dots and diamonds. The compact_test_representation_2 diagram presents the data using a histogram constructed from lines, text and filled rectangles. Hence, the `compaction_test` entity may be mapped to different geometrical entities such as dot and rectangle.

6.3.2.3 Mapping rules

After the mapping source and target are determined, there are still some issues about the mapping rules. Different mapping rules may be applied to the same mapping source and target.

For example, considering the graphical representation of the hole location attribute of the `hole` entity again. Presumably, the `hole` entity in the AGS model is mapped to the `circle` entity in the SVG model. The centre point of the circle is computed from the location of the hole, but the radius of the circle cannot get any information from the `hole` entity, and remains ambiguous and variable.

After the mapping source and target are determined, the mapping rule may still be variable.

6.4 The mapping specification in EMM

When representing an AGS file, different users will apply different graphical interpretations for different reasons at different times. The graphical interpretation of an AGS file is not unique and fixed. Selecting a graphical presentation style is dependent on the conventions required by the user and hence involves some interaction with the user. The whole procedure is shown in Figure 6.6. In summary, some configuration mechanism must be applied when considering the mapping to make an appropriate graphical representation selection.

Below is an excerpt of the mapping specification in EMM, which describes the mapping from the hole location to some geometrical entities in SVG.

```
Mapping UNIT ID: AGS_hole_location_To_SVG;
```

```
Container level:
```

```
    SOURCE: the location of a hole;
```

```
    TARGET: a circle OR a square corner rectangle;
```

```
Data Level:
```

```
    Source Data type: ags4.hole entity;
```

Target Data type: Svg_Geometry_Model.circle(if the TARGET's semantics is a circle) OR Svg_Geometry_Model.squareCornerrectangle (if the TARGET's semantics is a square corner rectangle.);

```
Mapping rules:
```

```
if dataTypeOf(TARGET) = Svg.Geometry_Model.cirle
```

```
then circle =
```

```
new Circle( new Point(hole.local_grid_x_coordinate,
hole.local_grid_y_coordinate),
```

```
default_radius);
```

```
if dataTypeOf(TARGET) = Svg.Geometry_Model.squareCornerRectangle
```

then squareCornerRectangle = new squareCornerRectangle (new point(hole.local_grid_x_coordinat-default_width/2.0, hole.local_grid_y_coordinate-default_height/2.0), default_width,

```
default_height);
```

From the above specification, it is clear that some configuration is needed. The mapping describes all the options; a hole may be mapped to a circle or a rectangle. Finally, some configuration should be added in to cooperate with the mapping specification to determine to which shape a hole is to be mapped. The configuration will help to specify what the target is on both the container level and the data level. It will also specify some default values for the mapping rules, such as the default radius of the circle and the default width and length for the rectangle.

The configuration has not been formally specified and studied in detail, because it is not the present research focus. However, some configuration related issues, such as formal configuration specification and its pluggability into the mapping specification, need further study.

The mapping specifications ideally describe all the possible mapping from the source to the target. Some configuration is used to determine and control the mapping.

6.5 Mapping Implementation

This step checks the correctness and efficiency of the above mapping in the practical Java implementation.

Figure 6.5 illustrates the whole procedure of translating AGS format data to an SVG representation. The finished software consists of three modules, the AGS parser, the AGS-To-SVG translator, and the SVG generator.

An AGS parser was created using JavaCC, which can interpret the AGS format file and create some AGS objects in memory.

The AGS-To-SVG translator scans the tree like AGS object hierarchy in memory, identifies the data nodes, which are compliant to the mapping specifications, and then generates a tree like SVG objects hierarchy with the identified data nodes.

An SVG file generator scans the in-memory tree like SVG object hierarchy and generates the appropriate

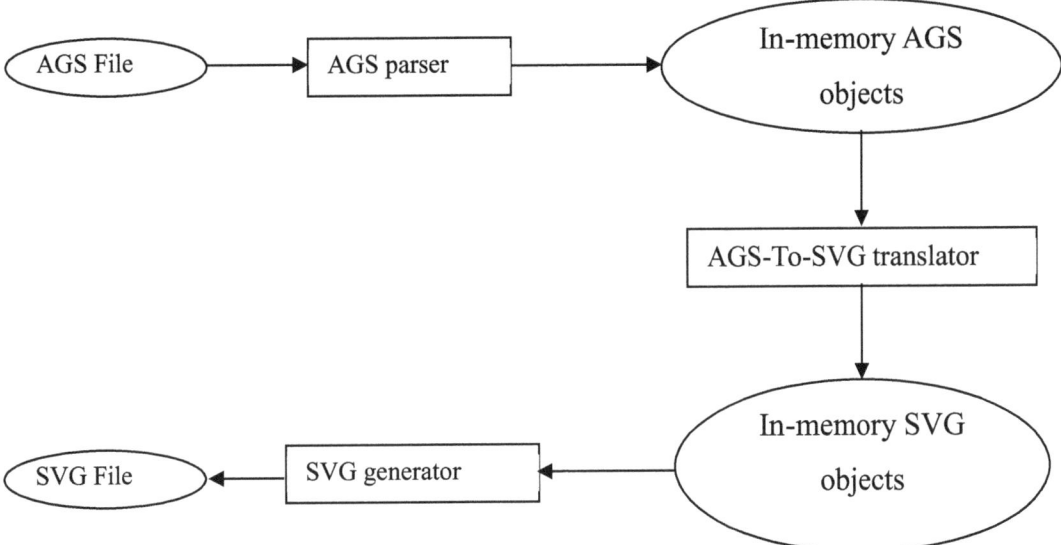

Figure 6.5 The Working Procedure of the Translator

SVG fragment. XML technologies such as DOM have been applied during this step in the same way as was done for Gerber to SVG. Finally, an AGS-To-SVG translator is successfully produced. Below are displays of data from two SVG files generated by the translator.

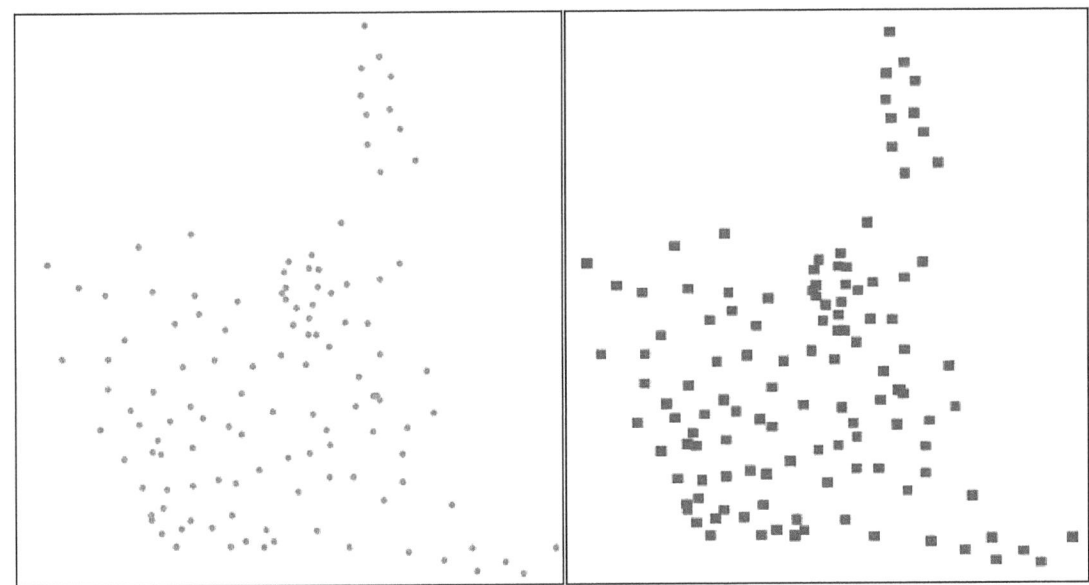

Represent the holes with circles   Represent the holes with rectangles

Figure 6.6 Translator Working Examples

Figure 6.6 shows two SVG images, which are the results of the same AGS data, which is taken from the KLICON Project [Klicon]. The image on the left represents a single hole by a circle, and the image on the right uses a rectangle instead.

6.6 Conclusions

The core of the AGS-To-SVG data translator is the mapping from the AGS model to the SVG model. The source of the mapping is non-graphics-related, whereas the target is graphics-related. The mapping involves selecting some graphical presentation and then identifying objects in the source model that can be mapped to objects in the target model that implement that presentation.

The experimental translator described in this chapter provided only a very limited number of examples relating AGS objects to SVG presentations and fixed configurations were used. The general solution to mapping between domains that are not well related requires further investigation. At a minimum, it is expected that a sophisticated configuration mechanism will be needed to control the mapping for this kind of translator.

Reference

[AGS99]   "*Electronic Transfer of Geotechnical and Geoenvironmental Data (3rd Edition)*", Association of Geotechnical and Geoenvironmental Specialists. http://www.ags.org.uk, February 21, 2002

[Amor97]   R.W.Amor, "*A Generalised Framework for Design and Construction of Integrated Design System*", PhD thesis, University of Auckland, May 1997.

[ASV]   The Adobe SVG viewer, http://www.adobe.com/svg/, February 18, 2002.

[Booch94]   G. Booch, "*Object-Oriented Analysis and Design with Applications*", Second Edition, ISBN 0-805-5340-2, 1994.

[Clark92]   S. N. Clark. "*TransformR: A Prototype STEP Exchange File Migration Tool*", National PDES Tested Report Series, NISTIR 4944, US Department of commerce, National Institute of Standards and Technology, 1992.

[EIA80]   "*Interchangeable Variable Block Data Format For Positioning, Contouring, And Contouring/Positioning Numerically Controlled Machines*", Electronic Industries Association Standard EIA-274-D. ANSI/EIA, 1980.

[EM95]   "*EXPRESS-M Reference Manual*", CIMIO Ltd, August 1995

[Gerber91] "*Gerber Format: Plot Data Format Reference Book*", the Gerber Scientific Instrument Company. http://www.gerberscientific.com/, February 21, 2002

[Gertrude] The GERTRUDE project, http://mint.cs.man.ac.uk/Projects/past.html#Gertrude, February 18, 2002

[Graphicode] GraphiCode, http://www.graphicode.com/, February 18, 2002

[Hardwick94] M.Hardwick, D.Spooner, M. Kilty, Z.Jiang. "*Mapping EXPRESS AIM's to ARM's Using Database Views: A comparison of Three approaches*" Technical Report 94041, Rensselaer Polytechnic Institute, Troy, New York, USA,

[IDEF98] IDEF1x Overview. http://www.idef.com/idef1x.html.

[IE]   Internet Explorer, http://www.microsoft.com/windows/ie/default.asp, February 18, 2002

[IJG]   Independent JPEG group. http://www.ijg.org/, February 27, 2002

[ISO94a]   "*Industrial automation systems and integration -- Product data representation and exchange -- Part 11: Overview and fundamental principles*", Reference Number ISO 10303-1: 1994, ISO, Switzerland 1994.

[ISO94b]   "*Industrial automation systems and integration -- Product data representation and exchange -- Part 11: Description methods: The Express language reference manual*", Reference Number ISO 10303-11: 1994, ISO, Switzerland 1994.

[ISO99]   "*PRODUCATION DATA REPRESENTATION AND EXCHANGE -- EXPRESS-X*

Language Reference Manual", Reference Number ISO TC184/SC4/WG11 N088, NIST USA October 15, 1999

[Jacobson92] I. Jacobson, M. Christerson. P. Jonsson and G. Overgaad, *"Object-Oriented Software Engineering – A Use Case Driven Approach"*, Addison-Wesley Publishing Company and ACM Press, ISBN-0201544350, 1992.

[Klicon] The KLICON project, http://mint.cs.man.ac.uk/Projects/past.html#klicon, February 22, 2002

[Latex] Latex Project Home Page. http://www.latex-project.org/, February 21, 2002

[MDA] Model Driven Architecture. http://www.omg.org/mda/ February 15, 2002

[Mint] *"Introduction to Information Modelling and EXPRESS"*, The Mint group Department of Computer Science, University of Manchester. http://mint.cs.man.ac.uk, February 27, 2002

[OMG] Object Management Group. http://www.omg.org/, February 27, 2002

[PNG] Portable Network Graphics. http://www.libpng.org/pub/png/, February 27, 2002

[Rational97] *"Unified Modeling Language (UML) Notation Guide"*, Version 1.1, Rational Software Corporation, Santa Clara, CA, September 1997.

[Rumb91] J. Rumbaugh, M. Blaha, W. Premerlani, F. Eddy and W. Lorensen, *"Object-Oriented Modelling and Design"*, Prentice Hall, ISBN-0136298419, 1991.

[SRP] SQL Reference Page. http://www.contrib.andrew.cmu.edu/~shadow/sql.html, Feb. 14, 2002.

[WEBGAIN] Java Compiler Compiler (JavaCC) - The Java Parser Generator, WEBGAIN. http://www.webgain.com/products/java_cc/, February 27, 2002

[W3Ca] Extensible Markup Language (XML), W3 Consortium. http://www.w3.org/XML/, February 27, 2002

[W3Cb] Scalable Vector Graphics (SVG), W3 Consortium. http://www.w3.org/TR/2001/REC-SV-20010904/, February 27, 2002

[W3Cc] Cascading Style Sheets (CSS), W3 Consortium. http://www.w3.org/Style/CSS/, February 27, 2002

[W3Cd] Document Object Model (DOM), W3 Consortium. http://www.w3.org/DOM/, February 27, 2002

[W3Ce] The Extensible Stylesheet Language (XSL), W3 Consortium. http://www.w3.org/Style/XSL/, February 27, 2002

[W3Cf] Naming and Addressing: URIs, URLs, ... W3 Consortium. http://www.w3.org/Addressing/, February 27, 2002

[ZN] J. M. Spivey, *"The Z Notation: A Reference Manual"*, Prentice Hall, 1989, ISBN 0-13-983768-X.

APPENDIX 1. `Svg_Geometry_Model` schema of the SVG model

SCHEMA Svg_Geometry_Model;

(*
** In this schema, the information of the basic shapes, path, text and the
** transformation of graphical elements are introduced. From the SVG perspective, a
** text is also a graphical element, even though what will be rendered actually is its ** glyphs in the selected 'font' element.
*)

USE FROM Svg_Structure_Model;
USE FROM Svg_Interactivity_Model;
USE FROM Svg_Animation_Model;
USE FROM Svg_Presentation_Model;
USE FROM Svg_External_Model;

(*
** This type models the number used for length value identification.
*)
TYPE valueSpecification = REAL;
END_TYPE;

(*
** svgLength means length, which is already reserved in the EXPRESS language, ** It consists of a number and a unit identifier.
** lengthValueInPixel: No matter what unit used, svglength is finally rendered to ** the screen in the unit pixel, so all subtypes have a common
**   attribute lengthValueInPixel to which they can be
**   converted.
*)
ENTITY svgLength

        ABSTRACT SUPERTYPE OF (ONEOF (svgLengthInPixel,
                                svgLengthInEM,
                            svgLengthInEX,
                                svgLengthInPoint,
                                svgLengthInPicas,
                                svgLengthInCentimetre,
                                svgLengthInMillimetre,
                                svgLengthInPercentage));
    lengthValueInPixel : valueSpecification;
INVERSE
    containingCoordinate : SET [0:1] OF coordinate FOR coordinateValue;
    containingRectangleWidth : SET [0:1] OF rectangle FOR width;
    containingRectangleHeight : SET [0:1] OF rectangle FOR height;
    containingRoundCornerRectangleRadiusX : SET [0:1] OF roundCornerRectangle FOR radiusX;
    containingRoundCornerRectangleRadiusY : SET [0:1] OF roundCornerRectangle FOR radiusX;
    containingCircle : SET [0:1] OF circle FOR radius;
    containingEllipseRadiusX : SET [0:1] OF ellipse FOR radiusX;
    containingEllipseRadiusY : SET [0:1] OF ellipse FOR radiusX;
    containingEllipticalArcCurveRadiusX : SET [0:1] ellipticalArcCurve FOR radiusX;
    containingEllipticalArcCurveRadiusY : SET [0:1] ellipticalArcCurve FOR radiusY;
WHERE
    ValidExistence : SIZEOF (containingCoordinate) +
                    SIZEOF (containingRectangleWidth) +
                    SIZEOF (containingRectangleHeight) +
                    SIZEOF (containingRoundCornerRectangleRadiusX) +
                    SIZEOF (containingRoundCornerRectangleRadiusY) +
                    SIZEOF (containingCircle) +
                    SIZEOF (containingEllipseRadiusX) +
                    SIZEOF (containingEllipseRadiusY) +
                    SIZEOF (containingEllipticalArcCurveRadiusX) +
                    SIZEOF (containingEllipticalArcCurveRadiusY) = 1
END_ENTITY;

(*
** This models the svgLength in the pixel unit. It does not have any private
** attributes.
*)
ENTITY svgLengthInPixel
    SUBTYPE OF (svgLength);
END_ENTITY;

(*
** This models the svgLength in the unit EM, which means the width of the letter M in ** the corresponding font.
*)
ENTITY svgLengthInEM

   SUBTYPE OF (svgLength);

   lengthValueInEM : valueSpecification;

   relativeFont   : font;

DERIVE

   SELF\svgLength.lengthValueInPixel : valueSpecification :=

lenngthValueInEM*relativeFont.fontFace.fontSelecting.fontSize.valueInSvgLength.

lengthValueInPixel/relativeFont.fontFace.numericValues.unitsPerEm;

END_ENTITY;

(*
** This models the svgLength in the unit EX, which means the height of the letter X in ** the relative font.
*)
ENTITY svgLengthInEX

   SUBTYPE OF (svgLength);

   lengthValueInEX : valueSpecification;

   relativeFont   : font;

DERIVE

   SELF\svgLength.lengthValueInPixel : valueSpecification :=

lengthValueInEX*relativeFont.fontFace.fontSelecting.fontSize.valueInSvgLength.

lengthValueInPixel/relativeFont.fontFace.numericValues.unitsPerEm;

END_ENTITY;

(*
** This models the svgLength in the unit point, and 1 inch equals to 72.27 point.
*)
ENTITY svgLengthInPoint

   SUBTYPE OF (svgLength);

   lengthValueInPoint : valueSpecification;

   relativeInformation : endUserInformation;

DERIVE

   SELF\svgLength.lengthValueInPixel : valueSpecification :=

lengthValueInPoint* relativeInformation.pixelsInPoint;

END_ENTITY;

(*
** This models the svgLength in the unit picas, and 1 pica equal to 12 point.
*)
ENTITY svgLengthInPicas
    SUBTYPE OF (svgLength);
    lengthValueInPicas : valueSpecification;
    relativeInformation : endUserInformation;
DERIVE
    SELF\svgLength.lengthValueInPixel : valueSpecification :=
lengthValueInPicas* relativeInformation.pixelsInPicas;
END_ENTITY;

(*
** This models the svgLength in the unit centimetre.
*)
ENTITY svgLengthInCentimetre
    SUBTYPE OF (svgLength);
    lengthValueInCentimetre : valueSpecification;
    relativeInformation   : endUserInformation;
DERIVE
    SELF\svgLength.lengthValueInPixel : valueSpecification :=
        lengthValueInCentimetre* relativeInformation.pixelsInCentimetre;
END_ENTITY;

(*
** This models the svgLength in the unit 'millimetre'.
*)
ENTITY svgLengthInMillimetre
    SUBTYPE OF (svgLength);
    lengthValueInMillimetre : valueSpecification;
    relativeInformation   : endUserInformation;
DERIVE
    SELF\svgLength.lengthValueInPixel : valueSpecification :=
lengthValueInMillimetre*relativeInformation.pixelsInMillimetre;
END_ENTITY;

(*
** This models the svgLength in the unit inch.
*)
ENTITY svgLengthInInch

    SUBTYPE OF (svgLength);
    lengthValueInInch : valueSpecification;
    relativeInformation : endUserInformation;
DERIVE
    SELF\svgLength.lengthValueInPixel : valueSpecification :=
lengthValueInInch*relativeInformation.pixelsInInch;
END_ENTITY;

(*
** This models the svgLength in the unit pecentage. The pecentage values are
** calculated according to the size of the referenced viewport.
*)
ENTITY svgLengthInPercentage
    ABSTRACT SUPERTYPE OF (ONEOF (svgLengthInPercentageX,
                                    svgLengthInPercentageY,
                                    svgLengthInPercentageOther))
    SUBTYPE OF (svgLength);
    lengthValueInPercentage : valueSpecification;
    relativeViewPort   : rectangle;
END_ENTITY;

(*
** This models svgLength in the unit pecentage, for X-coordinate value or width.
** Pecentage values are relative to the width of the referenced viewport.
*)
ENTITY svgLengthInPercentageX
    SUBTYPE OF (svgLengthInPercentage);
DERIVE
    SELF\svgLength.lengthValueInPixel : valueSpecification :=
lengthValueInPercentage*relativeViewport.width.lengthValueInPixel;
END_ENTITY;

(*
** This models svgLength in the unit pecentage, for Y-coordinate value or height.
** Pecentage values are relative to the height of the relative viewport.
*)
ENTITY svgLengthInPercentageY
    SUBTYPE OF (svgLengthInPercentage);
DERIVE
    SELF\svgLength.lengthValueInPixel : valueSpecification :=

lengthValueInPercentage*relativeViewport.height.lengthValueInPixel;
END_ENTITY;

(*
** This models svgLength in the unit percentage, for other length (not X-coordinate,
** Y-coordinate). Pecentage values are relative to: sqrt((relativeViewport.width)**2+
** (relativeViewport.height)**2).
*)
ENTITY svgLengthInPercentageOther
    SUBTYPE OF (svgLengthInPercentage);
DERIVE
    SELF\svgLength.lengthValueInPixel : valueSpecification :=
lengthValueInPercentage*SQRT(relativeViewport.width.lengthValueInPixel**2+
relativeViewport.height.lengthValueInPixel**2);
END_ENTITY;

(*
** This models coordinate. It is represented by an svgLength entity.
*)
ENTITY coordinate
    ABSTRACT SUPERTYPE OF (ONEOF (absoluteCoordinate,
                                    relativeCoordinate));
    coordinateValue : svgLength;
INVERSE
    containingPointX: SET [0:1] OF point FOR x;
    containingPointY: SET [0:1] OF point FOR y;
    containingPoint3DX: SET [0:1] OF point3D FOR x;
    containingPoint3DY: SET [0:1] OF point3D FOR y;
    containingPoint3DZ: SET [0:1] OF point3D FOR z;
    containingRelativeCoordinate : SET [0:1] OF relativeCoordinate FOR lastCoordinate;
WHERE
    validExistence : SIZEOF (containingPointX) +
            SIZEOF (containingPointY) +
            SIZEOF (containingPoint3DX) +
            SIZEOF (containingPoint3DY) +
            SIZEOF (containingPoint3DZ) +
            SIZEOF (containingRelativeCoordinate)=1;
END_ENTITY;

(*

** This models absolute coordinate. It is represented by an svgLength entity from ** the origin of the coordinates system..

*)

ENTITY absoluteCoordinate

  SUBTYPE OF (coordinate);

END_ENTITY;

(*

** This models relative coordinate. It is represented by an svgLength entity from ** the last coordinate of the referencing geometry entity.

*)

ENTITY relativeCoordinate

  SUBTYPE OF (coordinate);

  lastCoordinate : coordinate;

END_ENTITY;

(*

** Entity point only works as a defined data type, itself is not included in the SVG ** language, which means that you cannot draw a point in the SVG world. No

** definition of point can be found in DTD of the SVG language.

*)

ENTITY point;

  x   : coordinate;

  y   : coordinate;

INVERSE

  containingRectangle   : SET [0:1] OF rectangle FOR topLeftPoint;

  containingCircle   : SET [0:1] OF circle FOR center;

  containingEllipse   : SET [0:1] OF ellipse FOR center;

  containingLine_Start   : SET [0:1] OF line FOR startPoint;

  containingLine_End   : SET [0:1] OF line FOR endPoint;

  containingPathData_Head   : SET [0:1] OF pathData FOR head;

  containingPathData_tail   : SET [0:1] OF pathData FOR tail;

  containingControlledPoint_control   : SET [0:1] OF controlledPoint FOR controlPoint;

  containingControlledPoint_actual   : SET [0:1] OF controlledPoint FOR actualPoint;

  containingellipticalArcCurve_start   : SET [0:1] OF ellipticalArcCurve FOR startpoint;

  containingellipticalArcCurve_drawTo : SET [0:1] OF ellipticalArcCurve FOR drawtopoint;

  containingText   : SET [0:1] OF text FOR textBeginPoint;

  containingCursor   : SET [0:1] OF cursor FOR initialPoint;

WHERE

  validExistence   : SIZEOF (containingRectangle) +

                         SIZEOF (containingCircle) +

```
                        SIZEOF (containingEllipse) +
                        SIZEOF (containingLine_Start) +
                        SIZEOF (containingLine_End) +
                        SIZEOF (containingPathData_Head) +
                        SIZEOF (containingPathData_Tail) +
                        SIZEOF (containingControlledPoint_control) +
                        SIZEOF (containingControlledPoint_actual) +
                        SIZEOF (containingellipticalArcCurve_start) +
                        SIZEOF (containingellipticalArcCurve_drawTo) +
                        SIZEOF (containingText) +
                        SIZEOF (containingCursor) = 1;
END_ENTITY;
```

(*
** This type models numerical value of an angle, no units in consideration.
*)
TYPE angleValueSpecification = REAL;
END_TYPE;

(*
** This models basic data type angle in SVG. All concrete subtypes have a common
** attribute angleValueInRadian, because radian is the unit used in the
** EXPRESS language.
*)
ENTITY angle
  ABSTRACT SUPERTYPE OF (ONEOF(angleInDegree,
angleInGrad,
angleInRadian));
  angleValueInRadian : angleValueSpecification;
INVERSE
    containingEllipticalArcCurve : SET [0:1] OF ellipticalArcCurve FOR xAxisRotation;
    containingTextSpan   : SET [0:1] OF textSpan FOR rotate;
    containingTextReference   : SET [0:1] OF textReference FOR rotate;
    containingRotate   : SET [0:1] OF rotate FOR rotateAngle;
    containingSkewX   : SET [0:1] OF skewX FOR skewAngle;
    containingSkewY   : SET [0:1] OF skewY FOR skewAngle;
    containingDistantLightXY   : SET [0:1] OF distantLight FOR directionXY;
    containingDistantLightYZ   : SET [0:1] OF distantLight FOR directionYZ;
    containingSpotLight   : SET [0:1] OF spotLight FOR limitConeAngle;
    containingPresentationAttributesTextContentHorizontal :

    SET [0:1] OF presentationAttributesTextContent FOR glyph_orientation_horizontal;
      containingPresentationAttributesTextContentVertical :
    SET [0:1] OF presentationAttributesTextContent FOR glyph_orientation_vertical;
  WHERE
      validExistence : SIZEOF (containingEllipticalArcCurve) +
                    SIZEOF (containingTextSpan) +
                    SIZEOF (containingTextReference) +
                    SIZEOF (containingRotate) +
                    SIZEOF (containingSkewX) +
                    SIZEOF (containingSkewY) +
                    SIZEOF (containingDistantLightXY) +
                    SIZEOF (containingDistantLightYZ) +
                    SIZEOF (containingSpotLight) +
                 SIZEOF (containingPresentationAttributesTextContentHorizontal) +
                 SIZEOF (containingPresentationAttributesTextContentVertical) = 1;
  END_ENTITY;

(*
** This models the angle measured using the radiant unit.
*)
ENTITY angleInRadian
    SUBTYPE OF (angle);
END_ENTITY;

(*
** This models the angle measured using the degree unit.
*)
ENTITY angleInDegree
    SUBTYPE OF (angle);
    angleValueInDegree : angleValueSpecification;
DERIVE
    SELF\angle.angleValueInRadian : angleValueSpecification :=
angleValueInDegree * PI/180.0;
END_ENTITY;

(*
** This models the angle measured using the grad unit.
*)
ENTITY angleInGrad
    SUBTYPE OF (angle);

angleValueInGrad : angleValueSpecification;
DERIVE
   SELF\angle.angleValueInRadian : angleValueSpecification :=
angleValueInGrad *10/9 *Pi/180.0 ;
END_ENTITY;

(*
** SOME DEFINITIONS OF BASIC SHAPES
*)

(*
** Entity basicShape is the abstract supertype of all basic shapes, and its concrete ** subtypes are rectangle,circle...
** Mathematically, a basic shape is equivalent to a path entity in the SVG language ** that would construct the same shape.
** No corresponding element to basicShape is defined in DTD of SVG.
*)
ENTITY basicShape
    ABSTRACT SUPERTYPE OF (ONEOF(rectangle,
                                 circle,
                                 ellipse,
                                 polyline,
                                 polygon));
    transformSpecification   : OPTIONAL LIST [1:?] OF transform;
    rendered   : BOOLEAN;
    presentationGraphics   : presentationAttributesgraphics;
    presentationPaint   : presentationAttributesPaint;
    graphicsElementInteractivity : OPTIONAL graphicsElementEvents;
    eAnimation   : OPTIONAL LIST [1:?] OF animation;
INVERSE
    containingContainer   : container FOR eBasicShape;
END_ENTITY;

(*
** This models rectangle.
** If one of the width and height is zero, then the rendering of rectangle will be
** disabled.
** But the Adobe SVG Viewer 1.0/CSIRO SVG Toolkit, will still render it as a line,
** when only one of the height or width equals to zero.
*)
ENTITY rectangle

    ABSTRACT SUPERTYPE OF (ONEOF (squareCornerRectangle,
                                roundCornerRectangle))
    SUBTYPE OF (basicShape);
    topLeftPoint   : point;
    width   : SvgLength;
    height   : SvgLength;
DERIVE
    SELF\basicShape.rendered : BOOLEAN :=
(NOT (width.lengthvalueInPixel = 0) OR (height.lengthvalueInPixel = 0));
END_ENTITY;

(*
** This models square corner rectangle.
*)
ENTITY squareCornerRectangle
    SUBTYPE OF (rectangle);
END_ENTITY;

(*
** Entity roundCornerRectangle is the subtype of rectangle, which has its own
** attributes: radiusX and radiusY. Four ellipse are derived to describe the round
** corners. RadiusX and radiusY can be equal to zero, then the
** roundCornerRectangle turn back to a square corner rectangle, so
** roundCornerRectangle overlaps the scope of square corner ones.
** (the conclusion drawn out by experiment).
**
** The radiusX must be less than half of the width of the rectangle.
** The radiusY must be less than half of the height of the rectangle.
*)
ENTITY roundCornerRectangle
    SUBTYPE OF (rectangle);
    radiusX : svgLength;
    radiusY : svgLength;
DERIVE
    cornerDescription : LIST [4:4] OF ellipse :=
    [ellipse(point(
    coordinate(svgLength(topLeftPoint.x.coordinateValue.lengthValueInPixel+
    radiusX.lengthValueInPixel)),
    coordinate(svgLength(topLeftPoint.y.coordinateValue.lengthValueInPixel+
    radiusY.lengthValueInPixel))),

               radiusX,
               radiusY),

            ellipse(point(
            coordinate(svgLength(topLeftPoint.x.coordinateValue.lengthValueInPixel+
            radiusX.lengthValueInPixel)),
            coordinate(svglength(topLeftPoint.y.coordinateValue.lengthValueInPixel-
            radiusY.lengthValueInPixel+height.lengthvalueInPixel))),
               radiusX,
               radiusY),

            ellipse(point(
            coordinate(svgLength(topLeftPoint.x.coordinateValue.lengthValueInPixel+
            width.lengthValueInPixel-radiusX.lengthValueInPixel)),
            coordinate(svgLength(topLeftPoint.y.coordinateValue.lengthValueInPixel+
            radiusY.lengthValueInPixel))),
               radiusX,
               radiusY),

            ellipse(point(
            coordinate(svgLength(topLeftPoint.x.coordinateValue.lengthValueInPixel+
            width.lengthValueInPixel-radiusX.lengthValueInPixel)),
            coordinate(svgLength(topLeftPoint.y.coordinateValue.lengthValueInPixel+
            height.lengthValueInPixel-radiusY.lengthValueInPixel))),
               radiusX,
               radiusY)];
WHERE
   validRadiusX : radiusX.lengthvalueInPixel <= width.lengthvalueInPixel*0.5;
   validRadiusY : radiusY.lengthvalueInPixel <= height.lengthvalueInPixel*0.5;
END_ENTITY;

(*
** "circle" defines a circle based on a center point and a radius.
** The radius can not be negative. A value of zero will lead the entity to be ignored,
** not being rendered.
** SVG fragment, and the other entities will not be affected.
**
** The center gets a default (0.0,0.0).
*)
ENTITY circle

    SUBTYPE OF (basicShape);
    center : point;
    radius : svgLength;
DERIVE
    SELF\basicShape.rendered : BOOLEAN := (radius.lengthValueInPixel <> 0);
END_ENTITY;

(*
** ellipse defines a ellipse based on a center point and 2 radii.
** The radii cannot be negative. A value of zero will lead the entity to be ignored,
** not being rendered. But the Adobe SVG Viewer will still render it as a line.
** If radiusX equals to radiusY, the ellipse will be rendered as a circle. So ellipse
** overlap the scope of circle.(the conclusion drawn out by experiment).
*)
ENTITY ellipse
    SUBTYPE OF (basicShape);
    center   : point;
    radiusX : svgLength;
    radiusY : svgLength;
DERIVE
    SELF\basicShape.rendered : BOOLEAN :=
NOT((radiusX.lengthValueInPixel<>0)OR(radiusY.lengthValueInPixel<>0));
END_ENTITY;

(*
** line defines a line segment that starts at one point and ends at another.
** If startPoint equals to endPoint, the entity will not be rendered.
** (the conclusion drawn by experiment)
** And both points have a default (0.0,0.0);
*)
ENTITY line
    SUBTYPE OF (basicShape);
    startPoint   : point;
    endPoint   : point;
    presentationMarker : presentationAttributesMarker;
DERIVE
    SELF\basicShape.rendered : BOOLEAN := (startPoint <> endPoint);
END_ENTITY;

(*

```
(*
** Polyline defines a set of connected lines, in other words an open shape.
** Polyline can be self-intersecting and self-touching. (the conclusion drawn by
** experiment)
** If the values of all points in the attribute points are same, the entity will not be
** rendered. (the conclusion drawn out by experiment)
*)
ENTITY polyline
    SUBTYPE OF (basicShape);
    points              : LIST [0:?] OF point;
    presentationMarker : presentationAttributesMarker;
DERIVE
    SELF\basicShape.rendered : BOOLEAN := (NOT valueSame(points));
END_ENTITY;


(*
** This function is used to test a set of GENERIC data. If all the elements in the list
** are equal, it returns TRUE, else it returns FALSE.
*)
FUNCTION valueSame(data : LIST OF GENERIC) :LOGICAL;
    local
        result : LOGICAL := true;
        i      : INTEGER := 1;
    END_LOCAL;
    REPEAT UNTIL (NOT(result) OR (i>=HiIndex(data)));
        IF (data[i] <> data[i+1]) THEN result := FALSE;
        END_IF;
        i:=i+1;
    END_REPEAT;
    RETURN(result);
END_FUNCTION;


(*
** The polygon entity defines a closed shape consisting of a set of connected
** straight line segments.
** Polygone can be self-intersecting and self-touching. (the conclusion drawn by
** experiment)
** If the point amount is 2, the polygon shifts to a line, and the polygon becomes
** open. If the point amount is 0 or 1, it makes no sense. The SVG viewers ignored it, ** and some give a message that 'missing required attributes!'.
** If the values of points in the attribute points are same, the entity won't be
 ** rendered. (the conclusion drawn out by experiment)
```

*)
ENTITY polygon
    SUBTYPE OF (basicShape);
    points   : LIST [2:?] OF point;
    presentationMarker : presentationAttributesMarker;
DERIVE
    SELF\basicShape.rendered : BOOLEAN := NOT(valueSame(points));
END_ENTITY;

(*
**SOME DEFINITIONS OF PATH
*)

(*
** pathData is the supertype of all sorts of path data such as : zigzag, bezier...
** Each piece of pathData must have a head and a tail, so they are defined as
** the common attributes of the pathData, and they will be redeclared in the
** subtypes.
** And self-intersection and self-touching are legal in each piece of pathData, and ** among all pieces of them of one path.
*)
ENTITY pathData
    ABSTRACT SUPERTYPE OF (ONEOF(subPathPolyline,
                                 cubicBezierSegment,
                                 quadraticBezierSegment,
                                 ellipticalArcCurve));
    head   : point;
    tail   : point;
    rendered : BOOLEAN;
INVERSE
    containing: path FOR ePathData;
END_ENTITY;

(*
** subPathPolyline is a set of connected line segments,
*)
ENTITY subPathPolyline
    SUBTYPE OF (pathData);
    points : LIST [2:?] OF point;
DERIVE
    SELF\pathData.head   point := points[1];

        SELF\pathData.tail   : point := points[HiIndex(points)];
        SELF\pathData.rendered : BOOLEAN := NOT(valueSame(points));
    END_ENTITY;

(*
** controlledPoint is a couple of points, used to define a Bezier curve.

** Each Bezier curve must contain at least two controlledpoint, or it won't be ** rendered. Head is the actualPoint of the first controlledPoint, and the tail is the ** actualPoint of the last one.
*)
ENTITY controlledPoint;
    controlPoint   : point;
    actualPoint   : point;
INVERSE
    containingCubicBezier   : SET [0:1] OF cubicBezierSegment FOR controlledParameters;
    containingQuadraticBezier : SET [0:1] OF quadraticBezierSegment FOR controlledParameters;
WHERE
    validExistence   : SIZEOF(containingCubicBezier)+
                          SIZEOF (containingQuadraticBezier)=1;
END_ENTITY;

(*
** A start head, and an end point 'tail' and two control points define a cubic Bezier
** segment.
*)
ENTITY cubicBezierSegment
    SUBTYPE OF (pathdata);
    controlledParameters : LIST [2:2] OF controlledPoint;
DERIVE
    SELF\pathData.head   : point := controlledParameters[1].actualPoint;
    SELF\pathData.tail   : point := controlledParameters[2].actualPoint;
    SELF\pathData.rendered : BOOLEAN := NOT(valueSame(controlledParameters));
END_ENTITY;

(*
** A quadratic Bezier segment is defined by a start head, and an end point tail and one
** control points. This control point is both the control point of the head and the tai'.
*)
ENTITY quadraticBezierSegment
    SUBTYPE OF (pathdata);
    controlledParameters : LIST [2:2] OF controlledPoint;
DERIVE

```
    SELF\pathData.head      : point := controlledParameters[1].actualPoint;
    SELF\pathData.tail      : point := controlledParameters[2].actualPoint;
    SELF\pathData.rendered : BOOLEAN := NOT( valueSame(controlledParameters));
WHERE
    oneControlPoint : controlledparameters[1].controlPoint=controlledparameters[2].controlPoint;
END_ENTITY;
```

(*
** EllipticalArcCurve is a part of a ellipse, which starts at the starPoint,
** ends at the drawToPoint. The centerPoint will be calculated according to:
** startPoint, drawToPoint, radii and the X-Axis_Rotation.
** For most situations, there are actually four different arcs that meet to these
** constraints. Large_Arc_Flag and Sweep_Flag will decide which one to be ** drawn.
**
** xAxisRotation: The rotation, to the X-axis, of the ellipse as a whole.
**
** largeArcFlag: The arc sweep whether is greater than 180 degree or not.
**
** sweepFlag: The arc sweep whether in clock-direction or anti-clock-direction.
*)

```
ENTITY ellipticalArcCurve
    SUBTYPE OF (pathdata);
    startPoint      : point;
    drawToPoint     : point;
    radiusX         : svgLength;
    radiusY         : svgLength;
    xAxisRotation   : angle;
    largeArcFlag    : BOOLEAN;
    sweepFlag       : BOOLEAN;
DERIVE
    SELF\pathData.head      : point := startPoint;
    SELF\pathData.tail      : point := drawToPoint;
    SELF\pathData.rendered : BOOLEAN := startPoint<>drawToPoint;
END_ENTITY;
```

(*
** Each path entity consists a LIST of connected pathData and whether it will be ** rendered is derived from the rendered attributes of its pathData. It will be
** rendered if there is one or
** more than one piece of rendered pathData.
*)

```
ENTITY path;
   transformSpecification      : OPTIONAL LIST [1:?] OF Transform;
   ePathData                   : LIST [1:?] OF pathData;
   presentationPaint           : presentationAttributesPaint;
   presentationGraphics        : presentationAttributesGraphics;
   presentationMarker          : presentationAttributesMarker;
   graphicsElementInteractivity : OPTIONAL graphicsElementEvents;
   eAnimation                  : OPTIONAL SET [1:?] OF animation;
DERIVE
   rendered                    : BOOLEAN := whetherRender(ePathData);
INVERSE
   containingContainer         : container FOR ePath;
   containingAnimateMotion     : animateMotion FOR ePath;
WHERE
validExistence : EXISTS(containingContainer) XOR EXISTS(containingAnimateMotion);
END_ENTITY;


(*
** This function is to test rendered attribute of a LIST of pathData.
*)
FUNCTION whetherRender (data : LIST OF pathData) : BOOLEAN;
   LOCAL
      result : BOOLEAN := FALSE ;
      i    : INTEGER := 1;
   END_LOCAL;
   REPEAT UNTIL ( i>SIZEOF(data));
      result := result OR data[i].rendered;
   END_REPEAT;
   RETURN(result);
END_FUNCTION;


(*
** This function is used to test whether all pathData in a path are connected
** in the order which is clarified in the attribute ePathData of the path entity.
*)
(*
FUNCTION connect (data: LIST OF pathdata) : LOGICAL;
   LOCAL
      result : LOGICAL := TRUE;
      i    : INTEGER := 1;
```

```
    END_LOCAL;
    REPEAT UNTIL (NOT(result) OR (i=HiIndex(data)));
       IF (data[i].tail <> data[i+1].head) THEN result :=FALSE;
       END_IF;
       i := i+1;
    END_REPEAT;
    RETURN(result);
END_FUNCTION;
*)


(*
** SOME DEFINITIONS OF TEXT.
*)


(*
** Defined data type for the content of text, subTextElement.
*)
TYPE contentSpecification = STRING;
END_TYPE;


(*
** text entity consists of a single string, and some subTextElements, including
** textSpan and textReference,textPath.
*)
ENTITY text;
    content                     : OPTIONAL contentSpecification;
    textBeginPoint              : point;
    eSubTextElement             : OPTIONAL SET [1:?] OF subTextElement;
    eAnimation                  : OPTIONAL SET [1:?] OF animation;
    presentationGraphics        : presentationAttributesGraphics;
    presentationPaint           : presentationAttributesPaint;
    presentationFont            : presentationAttributesFontSelection;
    presentationText            : presentationAttributesText;
    presentationTextContent     : presentationAttributesTextContent;
    transformSpecification      : OPTIONAL LIST [1:?] OF Transform;
    graphicsElementInteractivity : OPTIONAL graphicsElementEvents;
INVERSE
    containingContainer         : container FOR eText;
END_ENTITY;
```

```
(*
** subTextElement entity must be in a text entity, but it gets its own
** presentation attributes. So the font of it can be different from the one of its parent's.
*)
ENTITY subTextElement
    ABSTRACT SUPERTYPE OF (ONEOF (textSpan,
textReference,
textpath));
    eDescription                  : OPTIONAL description;
    eTitle                        : OPTIONAL title;
    eMetadata                     : OPTIONAL metadata;
    presentationGraphics          : presentationAttributesGraphics;
    presentationPaint             : presentationAttributesPaint;
    presentationFont              : presentationAttributesFontSelection;
    presentationTextContent       : presentationAttributesTextContent;
    graphicsElementInteractivity  : OPTIONAL graphicsElementEvents;
INVERSE
    containingText                : SET [0:1] OF text FOR eSubTextElement;
END_ENTITY;

(*
** This entity can be rotated,
** validBeginPoints: The size of the list of characterBeginPoints, which is
** applied to its content, must be less than the amount of the characters in its content.
*)
ENTITY textSpan
    SUBTYPE OF (subTextElement);
    content              : OPTIONAL contentspecification;
    eTextSpan            : OPTIONAL textSpan;
    eTextReference       : OPTIONAL textReference;
    characterBeginPoints : OPTIONAL LIST [1:?] OF point;
    rotate               : OPTIONAL angle;
INVERSE
    containingTextSpan   : SET [0:1] OF textSpan FOR eTextSpan;
WHERE
    validBeginPoints : sizeof(characterBeginPoints) <= length(content);
    validExistence   : EXISTS(eTextSpan) XOR EXISTS(eTextReference);
END_ENTITY;

(*
```

```
(*
** The content of a text entity can be the character data of a reference
** entity. The other attributes are the same to the ones of textSpan.
**
** uriText: It is a reference to a text entity by its URI.
*)
ENTITY textReference
    SUBTYPE OF (subTextElement);
    uriText              : uri;
    characterBeginPoints : OPTIONAL LIST [1:?] OF point;
    rotate               : OPTIONAL angle;
INVERSE
    containingTextSpan   : SET [0:1] OF textSpan FOR eTextReference;
WHERE
    validExistence   : SIZEOF (containingText)+ SIZEOF (containingTextSpan) =1;
END_ENTITY;


(*
** textPath entity can place text along the path of a path element.
**
**  uriPath: It is a reference to a 'path' entity by its URI.
*)
ENTITY textPath
    SUBTYPE OF (subTextElement);
    uriPath              : uri;
    content              : contentSpecification;
WHERE
    validExistence   : SIZEOF (containingText) =1;
END_ENTITY;


(*
** SOME DEFINITIONS OF TRANSFORM
*)


(*
** This models the value identifier used in transformation.
TYPE transformValueSpecification = REAL;
END_TYPE;


(*
```

** This element offers a matrix, which can realize any transform after its application ** to the current coordinate system. It is inherited by some typical transform such as ** rotate, scale...
*)
ENTITY transform
   ABSTRACT SUPERTYPE OF (ONEOF(generalTransform,
                        translate,
                        scale,
                        rotate,
                        skewX,
                        skewY));
   matrix : ARRAY [1:3] OF ARRAY [1:3] OF transformValueSpecification;
WHERE
   validMatrix : (matrix[3][1] = 0.0) AND
          (matrix[3][2] = 0.0) AND
          (matrix[3][3] = 1.0) ;
END_ENTITY;

(*
** This models a general transform, which covers all other transform approaches.
*)
ENTITY generalTransform
   SUBTYPE OF (transform);
END_ENTITY;

(*
** It is a typical sort of transform, moving the geometry entities along the X, Y
** coordinates.
** It is valid to translate by 0,0.
*)
ENTITY translate
   SUBTYPE OF (transform);
   translateX : svglength;
   translateY : svglength;
DERIVE
   SELF\transform.matrix:ARRAY [1:3] OF ARRAY [1:3] OF REAL:=
                [[0.0,0.0,translateX.lengthValueInPixel],
                [0.0,0.0,translateY.lengthValueInPixel],
                [0.0,0.0,1.0   ]];
END_ENTITY;

(*

(*
** It is a typical sort of transform, scaling the geometry entities along the X, Y
** coordinates.
** It is valid to scaleX oy scaleY by 0.
*)
ENTITY scale
   SUBTYPE OF (transform);
   scaleX : transformValueSpecification;
   scaleY : transformValueSpecification;
DERIVE
   SELF\transform.matrix:ARRAY [1:3] OF
         ARRAY [1:3] OF REAL:=[[scaleX,0.0,0.0],
                               [0.0,scaleY,0.0],
                               [0.0,0.0   ,1.0]];
END_ENTITY;

(*
** It is a typical sort of transform, rotating the geometry entities about the origin.
** It is valid to rotate by 0.
*)
ENTITY rotate
   SUBTYPE OF (transform);
   rotateAngle : angle;
DERIVE
   SELF\transform.matrix:ARRAY [1:3] OF ARRAY [1:3] OF REAL:=
[[COS(rotateAngle.angleValueInRadian),SIN(rotateAngle.angleValueInRadian),0.0], [-SIN(rotateAngle.angleValueInRadian), COS(rotateAngle.angleValueInRadian),0.0],
[0.0   , 0.0   ,1.0]];
END_ENTITY;

(*
** It is a typical sort of transform, skewing the geometry entities along the x-axis.
** It is valid to skew X-coordinate by 0 degree and 90 degree, though skewing by 90 ** degree will cause the graphic element and its descendants disappear.
*)
ENTITY skewX
   SUBTYPE OF (transform);
   skewAngle : angle;
DERIVE
   SELF\transform.matrix : ARRAY [1:3] OF ARRAY [1:3] OF REAL :=
            [[1.0,TAN(skewAngle.angleValueInRadian),0.0],
             [0.0,1.0   ,0.0],
             [0.0,0.0   ,1.0]];

END_ENTITY;

(*
** It is a typical sort of transform, skewing the geometry entities along the y-axis.

** It is valid to skew Y-coordinate by 0 degree and 90 degree, though skewing by 90 ** degree will cause the graphic element and its descendants disappear.

*)

ENTITY skewY

   SUBTYPE OF (transform);

  skewAngle : angle;

DERIVE

   SELF\transform.matrix : ARRAY [1:3] OF ARRAY [1:3] OF REAL :=

                 [[1.0   ,0.0,0.0],

                 [TAN(skewAngle.angleValueInRadian),1.0,0.0],

                 [0.0   ,0.0,1.0]];

END_ENTITY;

END_SCHEMA;

APPENDIX 2. `Svg_Structure_Model` schema of the SVG model

SCHEMA Svg_Structure_Model;
(*
** The information described in this schema is about the structure of an SVG fragment;
** how it is grouped, organized, referenced, what external resources can be referenced
** into it...
*)

USE FROM Svg_Geometry_Model;
USE FROM Svg_Interactivity_Model;
USE FROM Svg_Animation_Model;
USE FROM Svg_Presentation_Model;
USE FROM Svg_External_Model;

(*
** 'container' is an element that contains graphics element and other containers as
** child element.
**
** eMetadata: It can contain a set of 'matadata', but it is strongly recommended that it
**   contains a single 'metadata', which appears before the other attributes.
**
** INVERSE: It is an abstract supertype, so the INVERSE attributes will be defined in its
**   concrete subtypes.
*)
ENTITY container
   ABSTRACT SUPERTYPE OF (ONEOF(svgElement,
                                group,
                                definition,
                                symbol,

                                pattern,
                                mask,
                                marker,
                                clipPath,
                                hyperLink));
    eMetadata   : OPTIONAL SET [1:?] OF metadata;
    eText   : OPTIONAL SET [1:?] OF text;
    eBasicShape   : OPTIONAL SET [1:?] OF basicShape;
    eImage   : OPTIONAL SET [1:?] OF image;
    ePath   : OPTIONAL SET [1:?] OF path;
    eSvgElement   : OPTIONAL SET [1:?] OF subSvgElement;
    eGroup   : OPTIONAL SET [1:?] OF group;
    eReuse   : OPTIONAL SET [1:?] OF reuse;
    eDescription   : OPTIONAL description;
    eTitle   : OPTIONAL title;
    eHyperLink   : OPTIONAL hyperLink;
    eAnimation   : OPTIONAL SET [1:?] OF animation;
    presentationContainer : presentationAttributesContainers;
    presentationPaint   : presentationAttributesPaint;
    presentationGraphics : presentationAttributesGraphics;
END_ENTITY;

(*
** Each container or graphics element can have a 'description' element, which will not
** be rendered.
*)
ENTITY description;
    eContent   : STRING;
INVERSE
    containingContainer   : container FOR eDescription;
END_ENTITY;

(*
** Each container or graphics element can have a 'title' element, which will not
** be rendered.
*)
ENTITY title;
    eContent   : STRING;
INVERSE
    containingContainer   : container FOR eTitle;

END_ENTITY;

(*
** Metadata is the information about a document.
** It is recommended that the metadata in a SVG document conform to the definition
** of RDF or Dublin Core (their specification can be found at the W3C website).
** A 'metadata' element is mandatory to the outrMostSvgElement entity.
*)
ENTITY metadata;
    content   : metadataSpecification;
INVERSE
    containingContainer : container FOR eMetadata;
END_ENTITY;

(*
** 'group' is a container element for grouping and naming collection of
** drawing elements.
*)
ENTITY group
    SUBTYPE OF (container);
    transformSpecification   : OPTIONAL LIST [1:?] OF transform;
    graphicsElementInteractivity   : OPTIONAL graphicsElementEvents;
INVERSE
    containingContainer   : container FOR eGroup;
END_ENTITY;

(*
** The 'definition' entity is a container/nest of referenced elements.
** It is recommended that referenced elements be defined inside of a 'definition'.
**
** INVERSE: Logically, the existence of a 'definition' entity is independent to the
**   other entities, so no INVERSE attribute is declared.
*)
ENTITY definition
    SUBTYPE OF (container);
    transformSpecification   : OPTIONAL LIST [1:?] OF transform;
    graphicsElementInteractivity   : OPTIONAL graphicsElementEvents;
END_ENTITY;

(*

(*
** The 'symbol' element is used to define graphical template objects which can be
** instantiated by a 'use' element.
** The difference between 'group' and 'symbol':
** a). A 'symbol' element itself is not rendered; only its instances are rendered.
** b). A 'symbol' element has attributes viewBox and preserveAspectRatio.
**
** INVERSE: Logically, the existence of a 'symbol' entity is independent to the
**   other entities, so no INVERSE attribute is declared.
*)
ENTITY symbol
    SUBTYPE OF (container);
    viewBox   : OPTIONAL squareCornerRectangle;
    preserveAspectRatio   : preserveAspectRatioSpecification;
    graphicsElementInteractivity : OPTIONAL graphicsElementEvents;
END_ENTITY;

(*
** Any svgElement, group, graphics elements or other reuse is potentially a template
** object that can be reused (instanced) in the SVG document via 'reuse' element.
**
** validReference: A 'reuse' entity can only reference to one resource such as reuse,
**   svgElement,group,symbol.
*)
ENTITY reuse
    ABSTRACT SUPERTYPE OF (ONEOF (reuseAnotherReuse,
                                  reuseSvgElement,
                                  reuseGroup,
                                  reuseSymbol));
    viewPort   : rectangle;
    transformSpecification : OPTIONAL LIST [1:?] OF transform;
INVERSE
    containingContainer   : container FOR eReuse;
END_ENTITY;

ENTITY reuseAnotherReuse
    SUBTYPE OF (reuse);
    anotherReuse : uri;
END_ENTITY;

ENTITY reuseSvgElement

    SUBTYPE OF (reuse);
    svgElemente : uri;
END_ENTITY;

ENTITY reuseGroup
    SUBTYPE OF (reuse);
    group : uri;
END_ENTITY;

ENTITY reuseSymbol
    SUBTYPE OF (reuse);
    symbol : uri;
END_ENTITY;

(*
** This type models the preserveAspectRatio in the model.
*)
TYPE preserveAspectRatioSpecification = ENUMERATION OF   (xMinYMin,xMidYMin,xMaxYMin,
xMinYMid,xMidYMid,xMaxYMid,
xMinYMax,xMidYMax,xMaxYMax);
END_TYPE;

(*
** svgElement is the top-level-element of the Svg_Geometry_model, which contain
** some graphical elements such as: text,basicShape,image and path. The transform,
** applied on it, will be applied on all elements in it.
**
** viewPort: It is the finite rectangle region on the canvas (conceptually infinite).
**
** viewBox: It is a rectangle region which is specified to map the bounds of the viewport
**   established by the given element. The methods of mapping, please see to the
**   'preserveaspectRatio' attribute.
** preserveAspectRatio: It indicates whether or not to force uniform scaling when
**   mapping the viewBox onto the viewPort. Please see the
**   Section 7.8 of the SVG specification for detail.
**
** transformSpecification: I tested SVG and found it is possible to apply a sort of
**   transform, such as translate, rotate... more than once on
**   a group of graphical elements or a svgElement.
**   It means that you can

```
**                    rotate a rectangle, and rotate it again, and again, though it is
**                    silly to do that.
**
** validInverse: If the current svgElement is an outmost one, which means it is the root
**               of an Svg fragment, it is independent of other entities. If it is not the
**               outmost one, then it must be a child of some other container entity, and
**               its existence is dependent on its parent.
*)
ENTITY svgElement
   ABSTRACT SUPERTYPE OF (ONEOF (subSvgElement,outMostSvgElement))
   SUBTYPE OF (container);
      viewPort                         : squareCornerRectangle;
      viewBox                          : squareCornerRectangle;
      preserveAspectRatio              : OPTIONAL preserveAspectRatioSpecification;
      zoomAndPan                       : OPTIONAL BOOLEAN;
      transformSpecification           : OPTIONAL LIST [1:?] OF transform;
      graphicsElementInteractivity     : OPTIONAL graphicsElementEvents;
      documentsElementInteractivity    : OPTIONAL documentEvents;
END_ENTITY;


ENTITY subSvgElement
   SUBTYPE OF (svgElement);
INVERSE
   containingContainer   : container FOR eSvgElement;
END_ENTITY;


(*
** The outMostSvgElement is the out most entity of an Svg file, it
** is the root of an Svg fragment, the parent of all other entities in the
** file. So its existence is indepedent of all other entities, and it must
** have a title and a zoomAndpan attributes.
*)
ENTITY outMostSvgElement
   SUBTYPE OF (svgelement);
   SELF\container.etitle          : title;
   SELF\svgElement.zoomAndPan : BOOLEAN;
END_ENTITY;


(*
** SOME DEFINITIONS TO: image
```

```
(*
** "image" entity makes it possible to render a image, which is stored in a file
** of such formats: PNG, JPEG and SVG, into a given rectangle.
** "uriImageFile" attribute references to a resource which contain the image.
** (See SVG Manual sect5.7)
*)
ENTITY image;
    imageFile                   : uri;
    viewPort                    : rectangle;
    transformSpecification      : OPTIONAL LIST [1:?] OF transform;
    graphicsElementInteractivity : OPTIONAL graphicsElementEvents;
INVERSE
    containing                  : container FOR eImage;
END_ENTITY;


(*
** This type models the uriImageFile, in fact, it should be the URI of a
** external image file.
*)
TYPE imageFileSpecification = STRING;
END_TYPE;


END_SCHEMA;
```

www.ingramcontent.com/pod-product-compliance
Ingram Content Group UK Ltd.
Pitfield, Milton Keynes, MK11 3LW, UK
UKHW060050240426
12048UKWH00019B/1414